Fear Regret Not Failure

The 7 Pillars of Success: "The SECRET to forging the mindset necessary to take risk, create wealth and succeed in an uncertain world"

By

Tony Velasco

Dorrance Publishing Co
585 Alpha Drive
Pittsburgh, PA 15238
Visit our website at www.dorrancebookstore.com

ISBN: 979-8-88683-507-6
eISBN: 979-8-88683-595-3

Table of Contents

Dedication

-No One Does it Alone-

Your mindset defines who you are. It affects your confidence, impacts your decisions, and determines whether you effectively pursue that which you desire most. It becomes the foundation of every thought and action you take.

The strength of your mindset, more than anything else, will determine your chance at success. Having a strong, positive mindset allows you to withstand failure and loss. It provides you the confidence to see past skepticism and doubt and gives a reason and purpose to everything you do. It is what allows you to overcome your fears and hesitations.

Possess a weak or negative mindset, however, and doubt will quickly replace confidence, invading your thoughts anytime resistance enters your world. Failure will be perceived, not as a lesson, but as a reason to quit. Struggle seen as evidence that you aren't good enough. With a weak mindset, you suddenly become much more susceptible to being confined by fear and crumbling under the pressure of life's challenges.

Your mindset is the foundation of everything you do. When it is well built, its strength can withstand any amount of weight placed upon it. A weak mindset, just as a weak foundation, will crumble when that same pressure is applied. The most important thing you can do if you're going to build something of value that will survive the test of time is to make sure the foundation upon which you build it is a mile deep.

"Fear Regret not Failure" will be that foundation. It will become the platform for everything you build. It will be the foundation that not only gives you the strength to withstand failure and loss but also to learn to welcome both because of the knowledge that accompanies them. It will provide you with the confidence to push forward when onlookers doubt you. It will give purpose and direction to everything you do. This book and the concepts contained within it are the fuel that will allow you not just to overcome your fears, but to leverage the power of regret to motivate you toward achieving your dreams and building a legacy worth remembering.

I assure you, however, that none of this is possible without one essential ingredient: people. And, more specifically, the strength and support of the individuals with whom you surround yourself. Achieving success is an impossible feat without help, guidance, coaching, and support from others. It is why surrounding yourself with people that make you better, that embody positivity, that hold you accountable, that challenge, support, and encourage you is of critical importance.

The strength of your foundation, and in turn, opportunities for your success will directly correlate with the types of people you choose to keep by your side. For it is the people closest to us who not only have the most significant impact on our lives but also give us purpose. They have the power to inspire us to pursue our dreams and passions and help forge the mindset that will be the foundation for everything we do. The people closest to us can either hold us back or inspire us to greatness.

Inspiration is defined as the positive influence or impacts a person, idea, or thing has on an individual or group. Most people draw inspiration from other people and their actions, which means that where we draw inspiration from is directly tied to our closest relationships. Who we surround ourselves with will either fortify our fears or help us to overcome them.

The power of these relationships affect more than our personal lives. Business, the economy, and our culture are all determined by human interaction. Our relationships can change our actions, influence our thoughts, and impact everything from our businesses to our personal lives. In short, our relationships not only dictate our lives on an individual basis but a cultural level as well. No business, no country, no economy, and no one person succeeds without guidance, support, and help from others. Anyone who tells you otherwise is either lying or has an entirely misguided sense of reality.

Maybe at no other time in recent history have these concepts been more tested. In 2020 and 2021 millions of lives were lost, economies decimated, and countries are now at war. The world is more divided than ever and we are on the verge of a global recession. Now more than ever is why these concepts are so important. Who you surround yourself with will be the ones that cultivate an environment that will either lead you down a path of succumbing to the negativity and fear of what lies ahead or push you to become something even greater in tough times.

Throughout my entire life, I have sought guidance and help from others and have been inspired by some amazing people without them ever knowing they were doing so. I have seen and felt love, heartache, success, failure, and struggle. I have learned from my experiences and became stronger because of them. For this reason, I would like to take a second to say thank you to all the people who have helped me throughout my journey. I want to thank everyone who gave me the strength to face fear head on, which is exactly what I hope to do for all of you.

First, I'd like to thank both of my parents, without whom I would not be the man I am today. Thank you to my mother for instilling in me compassion for others. You showed me what unconditional love looked like, and what strength and perseverance meant as a working single mother. Somehow, you balanced working full time while raising two kids. You took us to school, helped with homework, cooked, cleaned, and did everything else to run a household—all without ever breaking a sweat or complaining.

Thank you to my father for never allowing me to settle for less than my best, for teaching me what a strong work ethic is, for being tough on me when it was necessary, and always being there when I needed guidance. Thank you to my friends for your constant and undying support: Even if there were times you were uncertain of the risks I was taking, you were always there for me. Thank you to my business mentors, who impacted my life when you probably didn't even realize you were doing it.

Thank you to the entire team at Afterburn Fitness. We would not be where we are today without the contributions of each one of you. You continually raise the bar and amaze me day in and day out. Finally, thank you to my wife, who is undoubtedly my better half. Not only are you beautiful on the outside, but you are even more so on the inside. You will probably never know the impact you have had on me; just know that it is unparalleled. I cannot thank you enough for your constant trust, support, and encouragement. You are my rock, and everything I do, I do for you.

This book is for the people who have impacted my life, inspired me, and continue to do so. This book is for the naysayers and doubters. You fuel my fire more than you will ever know. Not just because it gives me the motivation to work even harder, but because maybe once you see it's possible, you will realize that not only could I do it, but you can too.

I only hope that this book can, in some way, repay all those who have helped shape the man I am today and, in some way, inspire you to chase your dreams. This book is about relationships and the power they hold. It is for anyone who is looking for inspiration and to better themselves just as I aspire to better myself every day.

Fear and regret are powerful words that have powerful meanings to me, and hopefully, by the end of this book, will to you as well. This book is about overcoming the fear so many people have that ends up suffocating their dreams. It's about understanding that regret if left unchecked, will haunt you later in life. This is about developing the mindset required, not just for you to achieve your goals and dreams, but to dare to dream in the first place. Most of all, it is about inspiring others to do the same.

PHASE ONE: THE PERSON YOU MUST BECOME

Chapter One: Liquid Courage

-Every decision has the power to change the course of your life-

I waved my hand in the air in desperation, hoping someone would see me. Nothing. I tried again to no avail. My adrenaline was pumping, my heart was racing, and my palms were beginning to sweat because the situation I was in was turning dire.

Frantically I began to look around for someone I knew, anyone. If I could just spot someone and make eye contact, I thought then maybe, just maybe, that would give me the opening I needed. All I needed was a chance.

There were bodies everywhere, making it difficult to move. I could have made a dash for the exit, but in my mind, that just wasn't an option. I needed to push ahead, and I needed to do it now. Time was running out, and if I didn't act quickly, all hope would be lost.

It was 1:25 A.M., and "last call" was in 5 minutes. The crowd to get a drink at the bar was so overwhelming I had just about given up hope, and then it happened, the opening I needed. I spotted a buddy of mine at the other end of the bar, getting ready to place a drink order with the bartender. I lifted my beer high up in the air and gave him this drunken variation of some combination of sign language and something resembling a "steal sign" a third base coach would give to a runner on first.

Most would have been completely lost as to what I was signaling to him from across the bar. Yet, without hesitation, my friend knew exactly what I was asking for without ever hearing a word uttered from my mouth. It's a language all our friends understood, of unconditional love and friendship; the silent gesture saying, "Beer Me!"

It was March in Tucson, Arizona, and just another Friday night at Dirtbags, at the time one of the best college bars in town. Yes, Dirtbags. Back in 2005, Dirtbags was the bar almost everyone who attended the University of Arizona went to on Friday night. There was nothing fancy about it (hence the name), but it had this fondness that no other bar in the area had. There was a large wooden oval bar in the middle of the main room at the entrance, but the room and the bar itself weren't very big.

Along with the small main room, there was a tiny dining area that was only large enough for a couple of tables, and a small outside patio. That's it. The stale smell of tequila shots, beer, and vodka almost seemed to permeate from the pores and cracks in the wood floors and walls, but to us, on Friday nights, Dirtbag was home.

It was nowhere near as large as some of the other college bars close to campus, nor was it nearly as nice or well kept, but this one held a special place in the hearts of everyone who went there. Simply put, going to Dirtbags was a part of the experience of those going to the University of Arizona. After all, their tagline was, "Dirtbags ... a part of growing up."

As special a place as it is for so many Wildcats, it holds an even stronger place in my heart. You see, it wasn't just that last-ditch effort to get a drink before "last call" that made that night special. It was what happened afterward that set the rest of my life in motion. The last-second drink order before the bar cut us off wasn't the only miracle in store that night. The truth is, I still had one last Hail Mary left in me.

The school year was about to be over. Come to think of it; my entire college tenure was coming to an end. I was in my senior year at U of A, and graduation was only two months away. College was one of the most memorable chapters in my life, and I was hell-bent on making sure the last couple of months would be no different. As I made my way through the sea of people to collect the beer my friend had so generously snagged for me, I bumped into a girl I shared a class with that final semester. She was cute, blonde, had blue eyes, and had a smile that could win anyone over.

As we crossed paths, we said, "Hi," chatted for a few seconds, and then both of us continued on our way. Now, up to this point, I would have considered us to be acquaintances at best. We were in the same class, would see each other around campus, and would occasionally chat when we ran into each other, but nothing more than that. I had always thought she was pretty, but we each hung out with our own group of friends, so our relationship never moved beyond being acquaintances. This was probably due more to circumstance than anything else.

That was until this night. This night I was fired up. I had just pulled off a last-second buzzer-beater, snagging a final drink before the bar cut everyone off, so I was on cloud nine. Well, that and I probably had some liquid courage going on. I figured I would capitalize on it and test my luck some more.

My best friend, Jay, and I were chatting on one end of the bar, and the blonde girl from our class was standing on the opposite side of the circular bar talking to some random guy. Jay also knew who she was. We had all run into each other on several occasions, probably had a drink or two together, and chatted in the past. However, outside of my telling him I thought she was cute, I had never really discussed any intention to try and pick up on her. Tonight, however, was going to be the night that changed all of that. I pointed her out to Jay from across the bar as I prepared for my next move.

To this day, I have no idea who the guy she was talking to was. I don't know if it was just a friend of hers or just some random dude hitting on her, but my intentions were simple. I was going to make my way over and steal her away from whatever conversation she was having and win her over.

What happened next is not a joke, nor is it an exaggeration of what transpired that evening. It is the God's honest truth, and my best friend Jay, who stood right next to me as I uttered the following words, would vouch for this entire story and its accuracy. Maybe it was overconfidence, perhaps it was liquid courage, but I put my hand on Jay's shoulder, looked him dead in the eye and said, "Watch this."

I turned and walked toward the other side of the bar. The bar was closing at 2 A.M., in less than 30 minutes, so it was now or never. I waded through the crowds of people standing shoulder-to-shoulder. Slowly but surely and confidently, I made my way through the masses, being careful to dodge beer and vodka sodas sure to be spilled if someone bumped into the person next to them.

As I got closer to my destination, I realized I had acted with such haste that I didn't have a plan of attack. What would I say to her? Would I pull up alongside her casually and act as if it were random, or would I just slide right in with confident intentions?

As I pondered these things, I realized I didn't have time to formulate a plan. Not only was the bar about to close, but I was also only a few feet away at this point. It was time to throw caution to the wind. I had to act. I closed in. The two of them were still engaged in a full-on conversation. In those last few seconds, I realized what I had to do.

If I was too subtle in my approach, I risked having her return to her current conversation, which seemed to be in full swing. I had to act boldly, and so that's what I did. Maybe it was the alcohol that gave me the confidence, perhaps it was the way she looked at me when we passed each other earlier, or maybe there was something else at play, but, as I took that final step, I stretched out my arm, reaching right in between them as if reaching for something on the bar they were leaning against. Then without hesitation, I acted as if I was surprised and happy to see her again.

"Heeeyyy," I said, giving her the standard one-arm hug using the same arm I just used to reach in between her and the guy she was talking to. It created a barrier and separation between them, allowing me ever so slyly to slide in between them. I parted the two of them just as Moses parted the Red Sea. My work wasn't done just yet, though, because I still had to come up with a conversation starter. I may have broken through the wall, but I had not yet secured the cargo.

I knew that if I was going to successfully hijack this conversation, what I said next had to be good. It had to be something memorable, something different—something clever. It was time to break out all the charm. "So, how'd you do on that test the other day?"

Okay, so, not exactly what I was hoping would come out of my mouth, and probably not the best conversation starter of all time, but only one thing mattered. It worked. She immediately engaged, turned her attention away from the other guy. He then turned and walked away. I was victorious. My swing for the fences move had worked.

Allison and I chatted and laughed the last 20-30 minutes before the bar closed. We exchanged numbers, and then quite honestly, the rest is history. Fast-forward 15 years and that blonde-haired, blue-eyed girl with a smile that can light up a room is my wife of over 10 years and has been an integral part of my happiness, and my success. You will hear me talk about her multiple times throughout this book because I believe she has not only made me a better person but a better businessman.

Fear and Regret

Allison is my biggest cheerleader and my rock. She supports me unconditionally while simultaneously calling me out on my bullsh*t to ensure that I always think of people before profits. She continuously gives me perspective. Whether or not she does it consciously, she consistently creates an environment that encourages success and all the risks I take. It is why I mentioned all the above in my Dedication. It's because she has not just shaped who I am as a man, but our lives as a whole.

So, then, this begs a serious question. What if I hadn't gone up and talked to Allison that night? What if the other guy chatting her up had asked for her number, and they started dating? What if we had never connected in that way before we graduated less than two months later? What if?

Allow those questions to sink in. I need you to understand the power that night has had on my life and to think about the potential alternatives to not doing what I did. I know I have thought about it. Let's be honest; if I had not made my move, there is a strong likelihood that Allison would not be my wife today. If I had not had the courage to go up to her that night (or any night for that matter), my entire life would be different.

I would not have met the woman of my dreams, nor would I have the partner that has co-created the environment for success I currently operate in. If she weren't in my life, maybe I wouldn't have had the guts to risk everything opening my businesses. Maybe I wouldn't have written this book.

Think about that, and more importantly, think about your own life. Ponder your missed opportunities. Take a deep look at how impactful every one of your decisions has the potential to be. Inaction has a greater impact on your life than you may ever realize. Fear, when left unchecked, is the killer of dreams. When fear is tied to rejection, failure, heartbreak, or loss, it will govern your decisions on whether to take risks. When fear takes control, it will lead you down a path of complacency, mediocrity, and ultimately regret.

Welcome to the entire point of this chapter and, quite honestly, the vast majority of this book; fear and regret. We are going to talk about a number of topics in the upcoming chapters, including success and what I believe are the necessary Seven Pillars to achieving it. But before we get into any of that, I'll set the stage with the one thing that drives me to pursue my legacy more than any other: the fear of regret.

I am not sure if my fear of regret was a subconscious aspect of the driving force that moved me to act that night in the bar, but I do know that it has been a part of how I have looked at the vast majority of the decisions in my life since I was about 12-years-old. You will find out later why that's the case, but for now, understand how powerful regret is and how much of a motivator it can be when you begin to fear and leverage it.

The full weight of regret only hits when there is a missed opportunity. If you talk to people who have regrets in life, it's almost always, not that they did something they wish they could take back, but rather that they DIDN'T do something. Missed opportunity because of fear of consequence is what stifles our chances to have the things we always dreamed of.

I could easily have opted for the safer, less controversial route, and not interrupted Allison's conversation that night. I could have allowed the fear of rejection to take over and convinced myself, as so many others do, that it just wasn't worth the risk of rejection. I could have allowed the opportunity to slip through my fingertips.

To me, there is only one way to look at opportunity, not just on that night, but every minute of every day: I would rather fail 1,000 times than wake up 50 years from now and wonder what if. I would rather lose and lose often than always wonder what would have happened had I stepped forward and taken the chance.

You see, this line of thinking isn't just about working up the courage to ask a girl or guy out at the bar, but also to confidently ask for a promotion. It's having the courage to walk away from the job you hate to pursue what you love. It's understanding that anyone who has found success at some point in his or her life, leaps. They leap without always knowing what lies below. They leap because they would rather fall than be left to wonder whether they could fly.

This is about legacy, your legacy. It's about living, knowing you have only one shot on this earth. It's becoming comfortable with failure. It's learning how to overcome your fear of failure with the fear of regret.

I want people to dream in the same way they did when they were kids, without limitation. Too often, we limit our own potential through some sort of elaborate excuse involving a skewed form of logic or reason. Most of us do this as a way to protect ourselves from whatever potential consequence lies on the other side of risk. All we really do when we think this way is guarantee that we will miss our chance at the things we want most.

Missed opportunity, more than anything else, will limit you to a life of mediocrity. To ever have a chance at hitting a home run, you first need to have an at-bat. To ever have an at-bat, you have to play the game. That means risking loss and failure. Sometimes it means starting all over.

To me, those risks are worth the opportunity even if I lose. They are worth it because I know all we ever have in life is a chance. Most people pass on chance or opportunity because they fear failure. They fear what people will say. They fear heartbreak or loss. Me? I know the only way to win is to risk losing in the first place. If I am going to lose, so be it, but I demand to have some impact on the probability of an outcome. I'd much rather go down swinging than watch from the sidelines.

You will never regret striking out swinging. You will, however, regret watching from the stands and never taking a chance. Fear one thing and one thing only: regret. Who knows? You may strikeout but you also might end up marrying the person of your dreams.

Chapter Two: Everyone has a Game Plan Until They Get Punched in the Face

-How mindset forms the foundation for success-

Boxing has been a hobby of mine for a good portion of my adult life. I played sports in school and have been active since I was a kid. At one point or another, I played baseball, basketball, football, and even soccer. I spent much of my life playing traditional team sports, but I fell in love with boxing the moment I first stepped into the ring. There was just something about the sweet science that pulled me in.

And while I've never had a professional—or even amateur—match, I've spent thousands of hours training, sparring, and competing since it became a hobby of mine years ago. Even without officially competing in a sanctioned event, I can tell you that there is something about boxing that makes me feel alive. The rush when facing an opponent is something you can't understand unless you have squared off against someone in the ring. It's a passion of mine that I continue to train to this day.

Boxing is a passion only surpassed by my obsession for business and entrepreneurship. I am the President and CEO of two companies, Afterburn Fitness and Gym Rev, a speaker, and now an author. Afterburn Fitness owns and operates health clubs in the Southern California region. Gym Rev is the most comprehensive digital marketing, branding, and consulting agency in the fitness industry today. We help gyms not only with their digital marketing and sales but also with building and curating their brands and visions within a framework of what we know works within the market.

Both companies were born from nothing. I do not come from money or a wealthy background. I received no inheritance, and I didn't win the lottery. Like so many other successful people, I started with nothing more than a dream. Long before Afterburn Fitness was even a thought, I walked door to door, placing handmade flyers created with nothing more than Microsoft Word and Clipart in the mailboxes of my surrounding neighborhoods for the fitness boot camp I was starting 15 or so years ago. Yet, after countless hours and tens of thousands of flyers placed on door handles, and in people's mailboxes (yes that's illegal, so don't do that), you know how many people signed up for it? Two. Two people.

Worth is Measured in Years, Not by the Hour

Why am I telling you this story? One, because I want you to understand how I got started. Two, and more importantly, I'm telling you this because most people would view two signups as a failure after handing out tens of thousands of flyers. Most would have decided not even to do the 8-week boot camp. Most would have gone with the mindset that it "wasn't worth their time" or that they were "worth more than that."

I, however, understood then and still understand someone's "value," when it comes to income or success, is not defined by what they make an hour or a day, but rather throughout their lifetime. It's about foregoing instant gratification for long-term rewards. It's about giving up the opportunity to have one marshmallow now so you can have 5 later.

I saw those two signups not as a failure but as opportunities. I had perspective. I understood that two were more than the zero I had yesterday. That's the type of mindset that so often separates the winners from the losers. That's the type of mindset you must possess if you ever hope to achieve the things you dream about. It's learning that the mindset required to succeed isn't that you are willing to do anything to succeed, but that you are willing to do anything even if you fail, just for an at-bat. Those two people were my at-bat, and I was going to make sure I did everything humanly possible to make sure I didn't miss.

The story goes that I didn't miss, and soon after, those two people became 5. Those 5 became ten. Ten became 50, and 50 became a company whose clubs now generate about $3 million a year each. Clubs that evolved into a digital branding and consulting company, speaking gigs, and now the release of my first book.

Understand and let that sink in for a second. I am not humble bragging. Instead, I share this to give you some perspective on how potentially impactful thinking positively can be. It's to show you that all of this started with just a couple of people—two people I could have bailed on. Two people that turned into a multi-million-dollar company with a lot more growth and potential still to come. Understand that we all start somewhere. Failure and disappointment are a part of the game. Sometimes getting knocked down is the only way to move forward.

The importance of this kind of thinking couldn't be more clearly illustrated than right now. While the shutdown orders will eventually pass, and the world economy will recover, there will always be downturns. There will always be recessions, turmoil, and unrest. You can either capitalize on them or succumb to them. You can complain and play the victim, or you can rise above it all.

A Competitive Edge

Whether it was playing sports as a child, working out for the majority of my life, boxing, or running a business based in the health and fitness industry, fitness has been a part of who I am my entire life. It should come as no surprise then that I share such an intense passion for both boxing and entrepreneurship. However, the similarities between the two extend far beyond just being an integral part of my life.

I have always been an extremely competitive person. Whether I am sparring, operating my businesses, or playing a random game of ping-pong, I play to win. It's my innate desire to succeed at anything and everything I do that drives this competitive edge. There is nothing I do without the desire to be the best at it. I have always believed if you aren't going to give your best at anything you do, then why do it at all? The natural competition of the business world, combined with boxing, is just something that feeds into the type of person I am. I enjoy being pushed. I am fueled by the challenge of battling back when facing adversity. I love when my skill and mindset are tested when my back is against the ropes.

The similarities between business and boxing, especially having the mindset necessary to succeed in either, is striking. Not just because both are sciences in their own right, but because both require a mindset that is willing to embrace and face the things we fear most. At stake are our vulnerability, ego, pride, failure, and fear, all in pursuit of success and victory. Both require learning to deal with adversity. It's learning how to deal with exhaustion, pain, and struggle while becoming comfortable with adapting on the fly.

Both business and boxing require understanding your strengths and weaknesses as well as your opponents. They each demand extensive training and perfection of a craft as well as thoughtful foresight, planning, and strategy. Business is the financial world's version of chess, and boxing is the combat sports' version. Each requires analyzing the competition's movement, patterns, habits, and reactions. Both are examples of competition in its raw form and can bring forth a powerful mix of emotions. They combine vulnerability and fear with power and absolute confidence. The combination of adrenaline, intensified senses and powerful emotions make for an unparalleled experience both in the ring and in the office.

The mindset necessary to achieve success in either realm is almost identical. Developing some measurable form of success in any facet of life requires that you stay agile and responsive. It will insist that you understand your strengths and weaknesses. It will demand that you be willing to take risks. You will need to learn to deal with adversity and failure.

But most of all, you will need to execute. You need to do all of this while managing the risk that things may not go your way, and reality will punch you squarely in the face. You need to be able to bounce back and continue pushing forward even if you lose.

These are the skillsets and the mindset to develop if you want to succeed. The importance of a confident, resilient, analytical, and prepared mindset is valuable in every walk of life. It will help you re-focus in your quest for more financial success and freedom. It will help you prioritize your health and fitness, which gives you more confidence and energy in everything you do. It will motivate parents to be better mothers or fathers and to empower their children to succeed as well.

Everyone has a goal. Whether it is to lose 50 pounds, to work toward that next promotion, or to raise children to be confident, kind, and successful people, everyone sets their sights on something. The problem is that most people never plan or train for failing. How will they deal with the idea that someone else gets the promotion instead of them? Motivation wanes when the pounds don't come off as quickly as they initially thought. Most people focus so intently on the goal or destination they forget to train for the journey where all the struggles occur.

Mike Tyson once said, "Everyone has a game plan until they get punched in the face." This analogy doesn't just lend itself to boxing; it's an analogy for life about mental toughness and resiliency. You either possess it, or you don't. Everyone will get punched at some point in life. You will get sh*t thrown your way. What separates the winners from the losers is not whether they can avoid the punch, but instead how they react to getting hit.

If you set out to start a business, at some point, you will struggle. You may not get the promotion you were hoping for, or even worse, you could lose your job. You could lose a loved one. You could invest your money and lose everything. Your country, or rather the world, could get hit with a new pandemic or war that not only kills hundreds of thousands but brings the world economy to a halt.

The point is, if you are not prepared to weather the storm, you will wilt when things stop going your way, and eventually, you will crumble under the mounting adversity. If you are not mentally and emotionally prepared to meet your challenges head-on, you will lose. Remember that so often in life, the winner is not the one with the most talent, but the one with the strongest will to win.

The Fires of Preparation

The concepts laid out in this book are first and foremost about success, your success. Not only will it help you determine what success means to you, but it will also outline what it takes to achieve it. It will provide you with the tools necessary to make yourself better one day at a time. In the chapters that lie ahead, I will go over how reverse engineering your decisions will change the way you think. I will show you the importance of defining your purpose and acting with intent in everything you do.

I will talk about how rewards do not come without risk. I will discuss the impact emotions such as fear, love, doubt, and regret can have on your decisions. You will learn to listen to, understand, and maintain control of those emotions. I will discuss the importance of self-awareness, knowing what you are good at, and how following what you are good at is more important than pursuing your passion.

As you read through the chapters, you'll learn the exponential impact positivity and enthusiasm have on your success. I will discuss the impact people have on your life and how important it is to develop relationships and people skills. I will illustrate the importance of grit, discipline and the importance of becoming obsessed. You will learn about the importance of time management and how there is no such thing as procrastination.

I will discuss how all these things tie together and create the Seven Pillars of Success: Intent, Grit, your Inner Circle, Delayed Gratification, Deadlines, Discipline, and Obsession. All of which are instrumental in your ability to learn to leverage fear so that you can begin to fear regret instead of failure. "Fear Regret

Not Failure" will do all these things, but by no means will it coddle you. If anything, this book will force you to take a long, honest look in the mirror to determine whether you are willing to do everything necessary to achieve success, because the truth is, most people are not. This book is not about making you feel warm and fuzzy; it's about laying the foundation for success. Understanding who you are and what you are good at will take you much farther in life than trying to be something or someone you are not.

This book will show you the real side of success. The one that involves working weekends instead of partying with friends; that illustrates the simple fact that eight hours a day just doesn't cut it; where lunch breaks don't exist, where you have sleepless nights worrying about the state of your business. It isn't pretty; it's the side that no one likes to talk about because no one ever sees it except the people who go through it themselves. This book is about developing the mindset and preparation necessary to deal with roadblocks on the way to achieving success.

Is this a get rich quick scheme or some kind of "lie-on-the-beach-and-collect-passive-income" fantasy? No. Those things do not exist in this world, and if someone tells you otherwise, they're the ones trying to sell you something. Remember, before you even think about going ten rounds in the ring, you must love everything there is about boxing— the good, the bad, and the ugly. Likewise, before you can be remotely familiar with success, you must love what it takes to be successful. You have to love the fight and the grind. You must embrace the struggles and the failures, and above all, you must have discipline. Without doing this, the possibility of having a fancy car or a beautiful house will not be enough motivation to keep going and push through all the roadblocks that will surely test your will. You will lose, and you will lose badly. It is the hunt that must drive you, not the catch.

Not everyone can handle getting knocked down. Not everyone reacts well to getting punched in the face, but these are the things we are here to train, so when they come, you are ready. Boxers willingly endure a grueling 12-week training camp to prepare for a match that will only last a handful of rounds. They do it to challenge themselves. They do it out of an obsession to compete and win.

It's not that fear does not exist for them; it's simply that they don't allow it to control them. They willingly embrace it because they understand that success is forged in the fires of preparation. Life is no different. You must train and prepare a lifetime for the single opportunity that presents itself years down the road. You must pass on immediate gratification for things that may only potentially benefit you years later.

There will be times when you want to turn and go back down another path, and that's normal. What separates success from failure is not that those thoughts enter your mind, but that you have the will to overcome them when they do. It's refusing to make excuses and play the victim. Only after you have endured the fires of preparation for your success will you be ready for whatever sort of punch life throws your way. You will know how to fight back and how to keep going, and that through perseverance, discipline, and the principles I teach you, you will walk away with the life you have always wanted to create.

Chapter Three: A Willingness to Fail

-The Seven Pillars of Success-

Merriam Webster defines mindset as "the ideas and attitudes with which a person approaches a situation, especially when the situation is seen as being difficult to alter." The most important part of that definition lies in the last few words, "especially when the situation is seen as being difficult to alter." Your mindset isn't something that's tested when dealing with success, love, or happiness. Mindset, by its very definition, is how a person will react and respond to adversity.

It's the first thing tested during hardship. It's the foundation for how an individual will react during times of failure, loss, and tragedy. Yet we frequently hear that we should train our minds for success. We read about having the mindset of a champion. And while I don't think the intentions of the individuals advocating this line of thinking to be misguided, I do believe the message itself is misguided when delivered in that context. So often, we are told to build a mindset around success when we really should be constructing our mindset around those situations that are difficult to alter. We should be training a mindset for overcoming adversity, not simply achieving success.

It is in dire situations like what the world just experienced with Covid-19 and the economic fallout that will likely follow it that we are truly tested. This time in our history will be no different than the stock market opportunities that existed after the crashes in 2008, 2000, or any time before that. Some people are panicking, exiting the market, or putting their heads in the sand hoping everything will be ok when they open their eyes. Other people are seeing uncertainty and fear as an opportunity. It's about looking for the positive no matter how dire the situation seems. It's about having a mindset that is constructed around the idea of perseverance and opportunity. There is an opportunity in everything; you just have to look for it.

Everyone is willing to succeed, but are you ready to do everything in your power and still fail? The problem with telling someone to build a mindset for success is that it presumes success. The reality is that you will fail many times before you succeed if ever at all, and so the first step in developing a strong mindset is to base it on anticipated hardship. That requires that you build your mindset around the presumption of struggle and failure, not upon success.

The average human life span is roughly 79 years long. That means, on average, each one of us will impact the world in one way or another for a total of 28,835 days. Depending on your present age, the number of days remaining on that counter is going to differ. Someone 20 years old has about 21,000 days left. Someone 30 years old has roughly 17,500 days left. If you are 40, you have about 14,000. The average person at the age of 50 has just 10,500 days left. The point of this isn't to be morbid; I mean it to give perspective in two ways. For one, it is to remind you that the amount of time we have is finite and how important it is that we make the most out of the time we do have. But two, it is meant to illustrate that no matter how late you start, you still have time. Even at 50 years old, 10,000 days is a lot of time to change your life and impact the world around you.

So many of us unknowingly give up on our dreams because we get caught up in everyday life. We forget about the things that inspired us to settle for security. We become complacent and forget about the aspirations we had once set forth. Most of this happens because of how we look at certain decisions. It's because so many of our choices are influenced by immediate gratification rather than long-term benefit.

It's because we dreamed big but never bothered to train the mindset necessary to battle the struggles we undoubtedly encounter on the path to achieving those dreams. When we dream, we tend only to think about the destination. Very rarely do we think about the journey itself and potential roadblocks and failures we encounter along the way. Most people never train or prepare for hardships and so when they encounter any resistance at all, they quit. "Fear Regret Not Failure" will provide the training to prepare you for those hardships. It will change the way you make decisions, it will encourage you to leap, and it will teach you how to fear regret over failure.

The Seven Pillars of Success

This book is organized into Four Phases and Seven Pillars of Success. Each phase has a dedicated concept and uses one or more of the Seven Pillars of Success to outline the path by which you achieve it. Phase One, which you are currently in, is about establishing the person you must become by diving deep into the first pillar of success; intent.

Phase Two is all about learning how to overcome fear using the second and third pillars of success; grit and your inner circle. Phase Three is centered around the concept of regret, your decision-making processes, and how to implement the fourth and fifth pillars; deadlines and delayed gratification into your life. The fourth and final phase is about the 1%, how you become a part of it, and how the final 2 pillars of discipline and obsession are the key to success.

So, let's begin, shall we? Before you learn about the other 6 Pillars of success, understanding intent is the foundation for everything. If you don't have a clearly outlined path, you will never know where you are going or how to get there. This is why Intent is the first Pillar of Success. Before we move on though, understand that intent is not simply the equivalent of finding your purpose in life. A lot of people confuse purpose and intent and although they are very similar, they are not created equal.

Yes, purpose can be the thing that gives you a reason to wake up every morning, but intent is how you go about actually executing everything on a daily basis. Intent isn't just the reason WHY you do something, it's the GOAL associated with the WHY and the habits formed around those two things that actually produces results. It's the idea that if you are a gardener or a landscaper, that you identify your long-term purpose of owning a landscaping company.

This is important because it will completely change the way you interact with customers, how you look at yourself, and how you operate on a daily basis. If your intent is just to go to a house to "mow the lawn" you will never become successful. But if your intent is to go to your clients house with the mindset that you are going to build a landscaping company, you will walk, act, and treat your clients and your services very differently.

What your intentions are will completely define your rate of success. We will dive much deeper into this next chapter, but just know that intent is the idea that you are intentional in everything you do. The second pillar of success we will discuss is Grit. Grit is the ferocity with which you relentlessly pursue your dreams. It is the result of having an emotional intelligence that possesses things like confidence, self-awareness, and perspective.

The third pillar of success is your Inner Circle. This pillar is about the influence the people you surround yourself with have on you. Understand the power your inner circle has. Understand the power relationships hold. Just as I talked about in the Dedication, the people who you surround yourself with will have a more significant impact on your chance of success than quite possibly anything else. To have any chance of success, you must change your surroundings.

The fourth pillar is Delayed Gratification. It is the understanding that to become successful, you must pass on what you want now in the hope of obtaining what you desire most down the road.

The fifth pillar is Deadlines. Deadlines are the only thing that forced you to complete a project or paper on time back in school. They are what keep employees on track, focused, and allow companies to grow. Deadlines are our only counter punch to the undeniable human trait of procrastination. Without deadlines, procrastination will rule your life.

Discipline is the sixth pillar we will discuss as it is the only thing that ensures longevity because motivation wanes. You will learn the difference between responsibility and accountability. And ultimately you will have to come to terms with the idea that your ONLY chance at success is to do the things don't want to consistently.

Finally, I will discuss obsession which is the seventh and final pillar of success. This quality quite possibly more than anything else we go over determines the level of success anyone can achieve. Together, all these things make up the entirety of "Fear Regret Not Failure." Something I learned early in my business that is important for you to understand is that while success requires a lot of things come together to make it possible, most of what success requires can be lumped into two categories: mindset and execution.

It isn't just success in business, but success in almost any endeavor. Mindset is a way of thinking; it's an attitude and the difference between approaching something with confidence or fear. It sees the same predicament as either possible or impossible. It's why one person can react positively to the same situation another person is negative toward. Mindset is how you approach almost every interaction, every conversation, every sales pitch, every interview, and every facet of your life.

The most successful CEOs and leaders in the world don't just have great tactical approaches to business and the systems they have in place to make a company run well. They inspire those that work for them. They change not just the actions of their employees, but the way they think. The greatest coaches in the world aren't merely great because they have the best offensive and defensive game plans in their respective sports. The great ones are great because they change how their players see the game. They motivate and inspire them to believe in themselves. They ignite a fire that other coaches before them were unable to do. Teachers that change students' lives aren't able to do so simply because they are the smartest or have the best curriculum. They have this impact because they incite passion and encourage their students to chase their dreams.

Do as I Do, Not as I Say

Yet, with all the power mindset possesses, alone, it is not enough; you must execute. Ideas and inspiration mean absolutely nothing if the action to complete them never takes place. Inspiration only lasts a short while. Habits form only through continuous action, and long-term changes take place only after new habits have been developed. That is the goal of this book. Not only to change your mindset, focus, and to inspire you to do great things, but to get you to go out and do it consistently and with purpose.

The concepts contained within the Seven Pillars of Success is how you should approach everything. It will impact how you approach work and your financial goals. It will change how you raise your children and the actions you take when you're around them. It will impact how you engage with the people around you.

Understand that we only have one life. To achieve the things we want, we must take chances. I want you to know that you should fear regret, not failure. I want you to live a life of positivity because negativity will suffocate your dreams. I want you to aim high and dream bigger than you ever have because it is much better to aim high and miss than to aim low and hit a bullseye.

I want you to understand that this world is about people, and the simple ability and desire to be kind is contagious. Smile and say hello to everyone you pass because you never know how it might impact a person's day. I want you to understand that life is not always going to pretty. There is going to be failure, loss, tragedy, and heartbreak, but the ability to turn those things into strengths is what will ultimately define you.

Chapter Four: The Power of Intent

-Defining your purpose-

What is your purpose? How do you define success? What are your goals and ambitions, financially, for your family, and otherwise? How do you want to be remembered? How do you want to impact the world? What is the life you want to live and the life you want to leave for your children? These are all questions you need to ask yourself, and once you have determined the answer to all of them, you have one more important question to ask yourself. Who is the person I must become to accomplish all those things?

If you are ever to succeed in life, intent must become the driving force in everything you do. Every move or action you take, every goal, every interaction, must be done with some kind of forethought of what you want to accomplish. And then, you must attack it obsessively.

While each pillar of success is important, Intent, just may be the most important. The reason is simple. None of the other six pillars are even remotely possible to attain without first establishing the driving force behind it all. If you don't first establish your why, if you don't understand why you aim to achieve something in the first place, there will be nothing to keep you motivated and driven when you undoubtedly begin to encounter life's challenges. If you don't assign a purpose to everything you do you will wander aimlessly and miss the targets you set for yourself.

Intent really breaks down into two central concepts. The first is the more commonly understood aspect which is defining your goals and your why. In other words, WHY are you doing something, what is your INTENT? The second part HOW you go about executing those things on a daily basis. This is the true long-term driver of success because it is the part that affects your every-day actions, develops habits, and establishes discipline.

Defining Your Why

Most people miss the single most crucial aspect of achieving anything in life: writing it down. Let me tell you that I have never accomplished anything in life that I haven't first written down. If you don't write it down or lay out a plan of action by reverse-engineering the path to get there, accomplishing it will not just be difficult but nearly impossible. I do this in every facet of my life. That's not to say that everything goes according to plan, because it seldom does. However, the only reason I ever succeed is that I write down what it is I set to accomplish in the first place.

I'm not just suggesting writing down your goals and ambitions. I'm suggesting taking the time to determine the thing that motivates you. It's determining not only your "where," but your "why" and "how" as well. Helping you lay these things out is what I will attempt to do in this chapter because once you have laid it out, once you understand what it is you are fighting for, it will become the motivation that fuels you.

Where are you going, why are you doing it in the first place, and how will you get there? The "where" is the destination or the goals you want to achieve for yourself and your family. These are financial goals, career-oriented ambitions, or other accomplishments you would like to achieve. The "why" is the driving force behind the reason you do what you do and what will keep you going through it all. The "how" are your day to day intentions and actions you deploy that will allow you to achieve those goals.

We are going to discuss all three pieces, but before we do, you first need to understand something important about behavior, how we make decisions, and how the brain works. Without this understanding, you will never be able to change your behavioral patterns completely.

Controlled by Fear

You see, most people will tell you that they are rational or logical when it comes to making decisions. If you ask them why they made a particular decision, most will rationalize that decision with a reasonable explanation. It doesn't matter if it is a purchase they just made, why they decided not to go to the gym yesterday, or the reason they haven't quit the job they hate just yet. The truth, however, is something far different, not based in opinion or theory, but based in science and biology.

As much as someone would like to have you believe their decisions are based on logic, it's emotion and belief that drive behavior. This is all true because we don't make decisions with the part of our brains that governs rational thought; we do it with the region of the brain which regulates emotion. This is something that has been studied for years and is a proven part of our biology. It's in our DNA, and there's nothing we can do to change it. One of the most-watched Ted Talks of all time and the one that essentially launched Simon Sinek's career was How Great Leaders Inspire Action in which he talks about this very concept. In my opinion, it's also one of the best Ted Talks of all time, so if you have never seen it, I highly encourage you to go check it out.

Sinek points out, as many scientists and researchers have before him, that the limbic system is the area of the brain responsible for all decision making. It's also the area of the brain responsible for all human emotions and all human behavior. What this means is that your emotions, behavior, and all your decision-making processes are intertwined. The part of the brain responsible for language and analytical thought, your neocortex, has no part in the decision-making process and is only there to rationalize your decision making. It's quite the sleight of hand trick. What happens is that since the part of the brain which governs behavior has no capacity for language, the other part of the brain that's responsible for analytical thought and language ends up verbally rationalizing our thoughts even though it's not linked to the decision-making process. What you perceive as logical decision making is verbal justification or rationalization of the decisions that have already been predetermined by your limbic brain.

Here's the scary part. Negative emotions impact decision making almost two times more than positive emotions. This means things like tragedy, loss, adversity, and failure impact your decision making twice as much as positive emotions like love or success. If that doesn't illustrate the importance of building a strong mind-set, nothing will.

You don't have to look far to find examples of this everywhere in our society. Why do you think every political ad is less about the great things a particular candidate is going to do, and more about telling you all the horrible things his or her opponent is going to do? It's because they know fear has a much bigger impact on decision making than inspiration does.

The news and media do this all the time. They drop a shocking or scary headline because they know that's what gets attention. They know if they want to get an agenda across because, let's be real, all media is biased now in some form, they do so by reporting statistics or information that incites fear.

Let me give you an example of how this fear process works. Imagine you are walking through the airport waiting to board a flight and decide to purchase a magazine to read on the plane. Let's assume you have a business or are contemplating starting one and so are looking to buy some kind of business or entrepreneurial magazine to read. As you walk down the aisle and look for something of interest, you come across two magazines. One magazine cover reads, "The 5 Things to do When Starting a Business," and another reads, "The 5 Things to Never do When Starting a Business." Which would you pick up?

Research says that an overwhelming majority of people would pick up the latter. Why? Because people are more concerned with the possibility of failure than they are with the likelihood of success. More people are worried about avoiding failure because fear drives decisions. This is precisely why you will see far more headlines or titles driving fear instead of positivity. Why does this matter? Because controlling these negative emotions will be critical to your success.

Until you learn to deal with those things well, they will dictate the way you act far more frequently than any sort of positive reinforcement or emotion. This is the reason most people are so quick to throw in the towel and quit when things get tough. It is why we try to rationalize our losses. We have a difficult time with things such as writing off bad investments because we are emotionally tied to the real reason we invested. And even though logically we know the right answer, we get sucked back in. Criticism and betrayal hurt so much more than praise and admiration feels good because of our emotional attachment. It's why one negative comment on social media affects people 100x more than ten positive ones. If you don't learn to control your emotions, you will lose and lose often. It's just how we are wired.

So if emotion is the primary force driving decisions, can you combat it? Do you have control over your decisions? The answer is yes, but only if you have control over your emotions. You may not be able to change your biology or how the brain makes decisions, but you can sure as heck leverage the emotions you now know are driving your behavior.

Leveraging Pain Points

The bottom line is that we all want to belong and connect with something. We want to be inspired. We want to be moved and understand our purpose in life. But we are also often fearful of failure, loss, pain, and rejection. Businesses and marketing departments understand this and use it to leverage human emotion for purchasing behavior. It's why determining "pain points" for customers is often used in sales techniques. But these techniques aren't just there for companies to make a profit, they are here for you to change the way you think, and it's why we are going to use them right now to define your purpose and to get to the bottom of what is going to drive you to success.

So, what are "pain points?" Pain points are emotional triggers that determine our actions and decisions. If you remember earlier, I talked about how negative emotions have two times more influence on a person's decisions than positive emotions. Pain points are a way for someone in sales to change a buyer's perspective on why they should purchase something or not by leveraging negative emotions like fear. This isn't a sleazy sales tactic like some would make you believe. Pain points allows us to understand true motives.

For this first example, let's use my company Gym Rev as an example. Just as a reminder, Gym Rev is my digital branding and marketing firm. We are a consulting firm for other gyms, studios, and health clubs. Our ultimate goal is to make gyms and their owners more money in an industry that has one of the highest failure rates. We generate more leads, sales, and revenue for our clients through an improved marketing plan, branding, and sales training.

Addressing a "pain point" is the reason a gym owner would hire my company in the first place. A "pain point" for someone in my industry might be something as simple as, "I am not generating enough leads or sales." Now if all we did was sell based on that, we probably wouldn't be half as successful. The reason is that type of sales tactic has no emotional tie to it. My sales pitch would be limited to something along the lines of, "We are going to come in and get you more leads so that you can generate more profit for your business. Our fee to do this is $2,700/month."

Of course, I am over-simplifying the message here, but you get the point. The bottom line is that I might get some people to bite with that approach, but because it's very surface level, it will be much harder to sell or close anyone. The reason is because that isn't my potential client's REAL pain point. The trick to getting to the bottom of his or her actual pain point is quite simple. I am just going to continue to ask why until I begin to uncover the real emotions that will drive behavior. Once I show you this example, we are going to do the same thing with you to get to the bottom of your pain points.

CLIENT: "I am not generating enough leads."

ME: "Understood; what happens if you continue to generate leads at your current rate?"

CLIENT: "Well, if I don't generate more leads, then I'm not going turn a profit."

ME: "What happens if you don't turn a profit?"

CLIENT: "I'm not going to be able to pay my bills."

ME: "What happens if you are unable to pay your bills?"

CLIENT: "I'm gonna have to shut my doors and might lose my house."

ME: "What happens if you lose your house."

CLIENT: "I don't know, but I can probably kiss my kids' college savings goodbye."

Can you see where we are going? The client's real pain point isn't that if he doesn't work with us, he might not generate enough leads, it's that he could have to close his doors, lose his house, and might not be able to send his kids to college. That's the real emotional driver. I am not there to sell the idea that we can get him more leads. I am there to sell him the fact that I can help prevent those other things from happening. Not only is it important because now I have a much better chance to sell him on $2,700/month in exchange for preventing those things, but he also will be more inspired to act once he takes a second to realize what's truly on the line.

Pain points aren't the only way to drive behavior. Granted, they elicit a 2X greater emotional response than positive emotions, but you can also use positive emotions like love, relatability, and stories of heroism to drive behavior. It just depends on your unique circumstances. You need to be honest with yourself with the questions. Here's an example of how that same scenario can be leveraged with positive emotions.

CLIENT: "I am not generating enough leads."

ME: "Understood; what happens if you continue to generate leads at your current rate?"

CLIENT: "Well, nothing bad, really, but I am trying to expand and grow my business."

ME: "So you are making a profit now?"

CLIENT: "Oh, definitely."

ME: "That's awesome! Ok, cool, well then why do you want to grow your business?"

CLIENT: "What do you mean? I want to make more money."

ME: "Yeah, of course, but why?"

CLIENT: "I want to be able to pay for my kids' college tuition."

ME: "Why?"

CLIENT: "Because I want them to be successful."

ME: "Why?"

CLIENT: "Honestly? Because my parents were never able to afford that stuff, and I want to be able to give them the opportunities I never had as a kid."

This approach makes it much easier for me to trigger a sale, knowing those emotional connections. It will also likely propel his willingness to follow through on the things I implement in his business because he is now looking at it from a completely different frame of mind, the same frame of mind I want you to build out right now. These aren't just tools for business owners and salespeople. They are tools for you. This is how you are going to build out your "where " "why," and "how" so that you can uncover your true purpose and take action with focused intentions.

So, the first part of this equation is going to be your "where," which is the destination. These are your goals in life. To keep it simple, you should break them up into three categories. Health, wealth, and family. Once you have those isolated, we are going to reverse engineer each of them to get the "why" and the "how."

For now, I want you to get a piece of paper and draw out something that looks roughly like the chart below. I have just a few random examples but want you to list as many dreams and goals as possible for each of those categories. Take your time and think about it. Don't rush the process. Take at least 30 minutes, but if you want to do this properly, you are going to need more time; plan on 30-45 minutes here and there over each of the next few days for a total of a few hours and if you have a spouse or significant other, get them involved in this process as well.

The reality is if you want any chance of achieving these things you both have to fully buy into it. I'll leave the choice up to you of how long you spend on it, but just know it's important. Also, be as specific as possible. The more specific you are, the easier it will be to reverse engineer the process on how to achieve your goals.

Okay, start that now and don't come back until you are finished. And remember, shoot high with your goals and aspirations. Remember that it's much better to aim high and miss than to aim low and hit a bullseye.

YOUR "WHERE" – Your dreams, your goals, your aspirations. This is the destination.

WEALTH	HEALTH	FAMILY
Become a VP at my job	Lose 15 pounds	Take kids to practice
Save 50k for kids' college	Go to the gym 3x/week	Have weekends off
Buy a vacation home	Lower my blood pressure	Make $500,000/year

Okay, now that you have compiled that list, I want to set the stage properly because this is where most people tend to stop when they draw out the things they want most in life. Most people stop short of the emotional connection when talking about goals and end up coming up short because of it. This occurs much in the same way salespeople, who only get to surface level pain points when talking with a prospective client, will fail to close.

When you ask most people what they want in life, they will respond with a lot of the same stuff you probably just wrote down or similar things to what I listed above. It's not that they aren't necessarily true, but the fact of the matter is, there are deeper reasons you want those things. Uncovering these reasons will elicit a much better emotional, and therefore behavioral, driven response.

You see, most of the random examples listed above (assuming your list is similar) will never motivate you through times of struggle. Not to mention, most of those aren't the real things driving you. Take the "Make $500,000/year" goal listed under wealth. I would imagine most of you stated some sort of dollar figure, whether it be an income or salary goal, an amount you wanted to have saved up, or something else. It's important to understand, however, that money isn't actually what you want.

You Don't Want Money; You Want Freedom

You might think I'm a fool for saying that but let me elaborate. First off, understand that you aren't alone. Most people are in the same boat. People think they desire money and wealth, but what they are really in pursuit of is something entirely different. Money is just a form of currency. We trade it for what we want. Money itself means nothing and is worth nothing. It only has value when it is exchanged for something we want.

What money represents is freedom. It represents time. It represents power. With enough money, you have no restrictions on where you can go, when you can go there, and how you get there. Those are the things people truly desire, and when we start to reverse engineer them, you will see what I am saying.

What you are going to do is ask "why" multiple times for every goal you state. I want you to stop and think about your answers each time you ask yourself why. There is no fixed or set number of whys you will need to ask yourself but know that a good number is between seven-10 times to begin to get a better sense of what emotional trigger is driving behavior. The deeper you can go, the better. Below is an example. Do this with each of your questions, and it should look something like this:

YOUR "WHY" – The emotional connection you have to each goal. This is your purpose.

GOAL Make $500,000/year

Why?

So, I can buy a bigger house and go on vacation.

Why?

Because it would be nice to have more space, a pool, and go on cool trips.

Why do you want to take cool trips?

Because I want to spend time with my kids and wife.

Why?

Because I want to be a good dad.

Why?

Because I didn't get to spend a ton of time with my dad growing up, and I don't want my kid to miss out on spending time with their father as I did.

GOAL Lose 15 Pounds
Why?
Because I want to look and feel good.
Why?
Because I'm tired of being overweight.
Why?
Because I don't want to end up like my mom who just passed away from heart complications.

As you can see, the real motivators morph over time. They morph into much more concrete and fulfilling objectives. They morph into motivators you believe in. And if they don't then it means you really don't care about them as much as you think you do. If you do this exercise correctly, after asking why enough times, you get to your real pain points. You get to the real emotional drivers or reasons for wanting to accomplish the tasks. These are your "whys." They are your purpose and will become the catalysts for getting to the "wheres."

The "wheres," or the destinations themselves, aren't bad. It's not wrong to desire wealth. Wealth provides freedom, which gives you the ability to grant your children all the opportunities you didn't have as a child. It's just that you need to understand that when you want to hit the snooze button on your alarm in the morning or when you want to throw in the towel, that you don't look at money as the thing that will motivate you to get up because it won't. You need to look at your children. You need to look at whatever your purpose is for wanting to provide them with the things you never had. Look at your "why" every time. That is what will allow you to persevere. Your purpose is what will let you wake up and get out of bed when the alarm goes off in the morning.

Finding your true "why" isn't always easy, and sometimes you find inspiration and strength from life's most significant challenges. The emotion that I leverage every day for my success was born out of one of those moments. What I am about to tell you is what drives me not to hit the snooze button. It's what motivates me to pursue what it is I dream of regardless of how many times I fail. It is what provides me discipline, and it happened when I was about 12 or 13 years old.

Fear Regret Over Failure

I come from an average blue-collar American family. My dad was a cop, and my mom split time between working and raising my sister and me. Growing up, things were tight at times financially, but nothing more than that of the average household. We weren't struggling by any means, but we weren't rolling in dough either. At one point, my parents, like many others out there, got divorced. And like many other divorce stories, it put a financial strain on my family. The height of the stress came at Christmas around 1994 or 1995.

Before the Christmas that forever shaped who I am, whether my parents could afford tons of gifts or not, they always did everything they could to make the holiday an over-the-top experience for my sister and me. My father, from whom I learned my work ethic, always worked extra overtime during, before, and after the holidays so he and my mom could afford Christmas gifts for everyone. The year of the divorce, however, no amount of overtime was enough.

My father was stern, confident, and direct. He was my "superhero," and to me was always bigger than life itself. He was the man I looked up to for advice, the man I feared when I got in trouble, and the man I aspired to become. He was all these things, but one thing he rarely did was show his emotions. My dad was calculated in everything he did and took pride in not showing weakness or vulnerability. Showing emotion could jeopardize that in his eyes, and so he always remained strong, even in times when most men would break. But even the strongest men break when it comes to things they care about. For my father, that was his children.

By the time Christmas came around that year, the divorce had simply wiped him and my mom out financially. For the first time in our lives, they had no money for gifts. I was well past the age of believing in Santa, so my father pulled me aside one afternoon to explain the situation. I can still recall the conversation to this day and vividly remember how the man who had never cried in front of me in my entire life broke down into tears because of his inability to purchase gifts that year. The idea that he was unable to provide for his children in that way absolutely crushed him. Perhaps he felt like he let us down, or that he was somehow less a man or father. It's hard to say what exactly was going through his head at that time, but all I know is, in the 40 years I have been alive, this was, and still is, the only time I have ever seen my father cry.

Something so simple, so inconsequential, so unimportant in the grand scheme of things, destroyed the man whose demeanor and confidence formerly made me feel like I was in the presence of a giant. At the time, I didn't fully understand why something so unimportant was making him cry. All I knew was that I saw such awful pain in his eyes.

That moment has been seared into my memory for my entire life and is part of what drives me so hard every single day. I understand that there will always be unforeseen circumstances that will be out of my control. I understand that one cannot plan for all the curveballs life throws. But if there is one thing I can control, it's doing everything in my power to TRY and prevent something like what happened to my dad from ever happening to me. And if by some chance it does, that I will still be able to look myself in the mirror and know without a shadow of a doubt that I did all I could.

The thing I will never allow myself to experience is the feeling of regret that I could have done something more. I never want to have to experience what he did that day. It's that fear of regret that pushes me every day, not just from a financial stability point, but also to be a better man. Not getting Christmas gifts that year didn't matter to me. I couldn't have cared less, but to my father, it was everything. I can imagine it would be that way for any father. That experience, and my desire to never have to be in his shoes and feel the same pain he did, is part of what drives me every day. It is my driving force, it is the motto I live by, and it is why the book is called "Fear Regret Not Failure."

If I had listed my specific financial goals, and I had reverse-engineered that example above, the story I just told you is what would have come from it. For me, financial wealth and stability are broken down into a "why" that encompasses my fear of regret. Regret that if I didn't pursue the things I desired most with absolute vigor, I would potentially be putting myself in harm's way for the same circumstance to happen to me. That is something I just will not allow, and so it is how I operate every day of my life now because of it.

The fear of regret invades every aspect of my life, and it is the single, most powerful emotion I use to leverage for success. I fear waking up 30 years from now wondering, "what if." I fear that one day I will wonder if I could have done better for my family. I fear that lying on my death bed; I will wish I had done more for society or the world as a whole. And so, I live my life in a way that I never allow an opportunity to potentially feel that way 10, 20, 50 years down the road. I operate in a way that leaves no doubt. It doesn't matter if I fail at something; I just want to know that I have done everything I possibly could. I will leave no stone unturned. I do that because I understand that I have one shot here on earth and will not waste one minute because of it. I won't ever not take chances because of a fear of failing.

I will never sleep on an opportunity. I will die trying to provide the life for my family, both financially and otherwise. I will only rest easy, knowing that I did everything in my power to provide the best life possible. The reality is you will either feel pain and discomfort from the struggle and failure that must occur on the path to success or you will feel pain and discomfort from the regret of never giving it a shot. You choose.

This is how success is achieved. This is what success is. Success isn't money or wealth like most would have you believe. Success is happiness. Success is the accomplishment of an aim or purpose. Success is the pursuit of the thing that gives you a reason to wake up every day.

The Person You Must Become

In the very beginning on this chapter, I asked a question. Who is the person you must become to accomplish everything you set out to achieve? I really need you to think about this because your success or failure will hinge on your ability to change who you are. We have defined the "where" and the "why." Now it is time to define the "how."

The "how" is the person you must become to see those things through. Most people when they speak of intent or purpose, they just think of the thing that drives them. That's the part we just spent that vast majority of this chapter discussing, but we are going to end it with the part that is even more important. The actions you take on a daily basis to get there.

This is more than just what you do with your time. It is the intent or purpose tied to those specific actions. Intent is important not just because it gives purpose and meaning to everything you do, but because it will change how you do it. Let me explain.

If you're a personal trainer with ambitions of opening up your own studio or club, then you can't simply treat your clients as clients. You should treat them as members. You will deliver a much better product and customer experience to them than if you were to just see yourself as a personal trainer.

If you are bartender with a dream of opening your own restaurant or bar, or starting a YouTube channel, and you operate with that intent every single day. You will make much greater strides in accomplishing that goal than just "pouring people's drinks." You will find more ways to be creative, to stand out, to provide a better experience, and to learn some of the other elements to the restaurant business. If you are a hair stylist with the goal of opening your own salon then you will need to increase your customer base and save money with a completely different level of intent than the person who just "cuts hair."

The point is intent matters because your intentions are what will drive the "how," or the path by which you accomplish your "where." Intent is the trajectory you set yourself on to accomplish your goals on a daily basis. It will change how you look at client interactions. It will change how you look at margins, follow up, returns, referrals, training and more.

It's about looking at things with a broader stroke versus just the task itself. If you act with intent, then you will no longer simply "mow someone's lawn." You will understand your worth and your purpose encompasses far more than that. You will interact with your client better, you will deliver a better product and customer experience, you will follow up better. You will change the title of what you do from "gardener" to "landscape architect." You may laugh and think it's just a false title, but you'd be wrong because perception in this world is everything. And not just how a potential client perceives you because of your title, but more importantly because of how you will perceive yourself.

Perspective is a Superpower

Perspective extends far beyond client interactions and how you look at yourself. It will also have a huge impact on how you look at the world as a whole. I feel I have been given a gift by being born in a country like the United States, where I am free. I feel an obligation not to waste the opportunities afforded to me. There are billions of people on this planet, the vast majority of whom are born in countries where opportunity doesn't exist. Some people live in constant fear of terrorism or are forced to live off pennies a day. We forget that if you are reading this book, it means that you are more than likely a part of the top 1% of the world.

To be a part of the 1% in the world, you only need to make around $37,000/year. You heard right. If you make more than 37k per year, you are wealthier than 99% of the people in this world. Let that sink in for a bit. I want you to contemplate for a minute all the things you complain about. I want you to think about Monday mornings when you complain about the work week ahead. I want you to think about the length of the Starbucks line that irritated you this morning. I want you to have perspective. I want you to think about how no matter how hard and unfair life may seem at times, you still live in a country where opportunity exists at every corner.

Think about the billions of people who live in a state of poverty that most of us can't even comprehend. Two-thirds of the world's population lives on less than $2/day. There are people who live in fear every single day because of religious, sexual, racial, or ethnic persecution. I want to make sure you understand that if you are reading this book, you are in the minority. You, like myself, are the lucky ones.

With Coronavirus, without Coronavirus, or whatever else the world throws at you, there is still opportunity at every corner. It's just whether you look for it or not. You can complain, or you can do. It's as simple as that. Purpose, intent, and perspective matter. Not only because they act as goal posts for your life's journey, but because they will be the fuel required to overcome life's challenges. To succeed you will need perseverance and determination. You will need grit. You will need to embrace the suck.

PHASE TWO: OVERCOMING FEAR

Chapter Five: Embrace the Suck

-Grit and the fearlessness required to succeed-

If there were a group of people who embodied the term Grit, the Navy SEALs would definitely be it. Afterall they are one of the most elite military units in the world. They were responsible for executing one of the most covert military operations in US history taking out Osama Bin Laden himself. But covert military operations aside, one of the things they are most heralded for is their training process. A process that eliminates over 90% of its highly capable participants. BUDS, which stands for Basic Underwater Demolition/SEAL is the first 6 months of an 18-month training process to become a SEAL. 90% of everyone that embarks on that 6-month BUDS process quits before it's over.

The entire BUDS training is demanding for sure, but one week in particular stands out from the rest. The third week of BUDS is known as Hell Week and is designed for one thing and one thing only. To weed out those who lack the commitment or mindset necessary to make it through the training. Participants barely sleep for a week, they run hundreds and swim dozens of miles in frigid water, endure brutal beatings, and are brought to the brink of complete mental and physical breakdown. They are quite literally urged to quit at every corner.

You would think that only the toughest, strongest, and most fit individuals would be the ones that make up the 10% that make it through the training. You'd be wrong. Talk to anyone that has actually made it through the process and they will tell you that the biggest, baddest, and strongest individuals are often the first to go.

The ones who actually make it through are not the ones who are physically the toughest, but instead the ones whose mindsets are the most resilient. The individuals whose mindset allows them to overcome pain, exhaustion, and a never-ending feeling of defeat are the ones who make it to the finish line. The participants who are able to overcome struggle, hardship, and discomfort are the ones who make the cut. The SEALs are quite literally formed through adversity.

The crazy thing is that people who make it through aren't special any way. They are just the ones who have an uncommon desire to be great. This is no different than your quest for success or greatness in your own realm. Your ability to overcome adversity with grit and perseverance is the common denominator for success, just as it is for a Navy SEAL. The differentiating factor that separates the ones who succeed from the ones who quit is that the ones who make it, "Embrace the suck" as the Navy SEALs say. They understand just as Martin Luther King did:

> "If you can't fly then run.
> If you can't run then walk.
> If you can't walk, then crawl.
> But whatever you do, you have to keep moving forward."

Grit is to act in defiance of anything that stands in your way. It is pure unadulterated determination, no matter the circumstances one encounters. Grit, simply put, is one's ability to overcome. It's the second of the Seven Pillars of Success, and according to several studies, is the most commonly held trait amongst successful people.

Welcome to Phase Two: Overcoming Fear. The first four chapters in Phase One were about laying the groundwork of your mindset and the importance of acting with intent in everything you do. In this phase, we will look at how the second and third pillars of success, grit, and your inner circle, combine to form the foundation for your ability to overcome the one thing that prevents 99 percent of people from achieving their dreams aspirations. Fear.

In her book appropriately titled, Grit, Angela Duckworth talks about how grit is the single most significant predictor of success, more than IQ, social intelligence, or anything else they controlled for. In other words, you need grit if you want any chance of succeeding in life. The question is, how do you get it? Or maybe more importantly, why do some people seem to possess the fire and determination necessary to succeed, and some don't? What allows some to make it through BUDS while others break? What gives them that ability to power through struggle and adversity while others wilt under pressure?

These sorts of things are magnified during difficult times, like what we've experienced from 2020 through now (2022). Think about how much of what has transpired that is out of our control. During the Coronavirus lockdowns, people were forced out of work, businesses required to shut down, and everyday people told to stay home. Regardless of whether you agreed with how things were handled is irrelevant. The bottom line is that these are the kind of things in life that are completely out of our control. Which is precisely why retaining a positive and strong frame of mind is so important.

#Hustle is more than a hashtag

The reality is nothing matters if you don't execute. Most people have no clue what it "hustle" actually means. Most people "think" they hustle, but they don't. They claim to hustle on Instagram and Facebook with hashtags, but it's a façade. They do it because it's cool to #hustle and #grind, but most reading this have no idea what it's like to work 80+ hours a week. Far too many people consider anything over 40 hours a week "hustling."

Many people reading this don't know what it's like to work weekends. Most will complain they don't have time to work out or time to pursue a side venture, but the reality is that they are choosing not to. Most feed themselves bullsh*t. Most make excuses for why they can't do something, but the bottom line is that real hustle doesn't make excuses. Real hustle just does whatever is necessary to accomplish the goal at hand.

It's time to look in the mirror and ask yourself if you could sleep six hours instead of eight. It's time to ask yourself if you watch TV at all during the week. It's time to ask yourself if you play video games, or if you waste time blindly consuming content on Facebook, YouTube, Instagram, or Tik Tok. It's time to ask yourself if you choose to party or hang out with your friends on the weekend instead of working toward your dreams.

Look, there's nothing wrong with doing any of that if you just want to live a mediocre and complacent life. If however you wrote down some ridiculous goals, you sure as hell better have some ridiculous plans on how to get there. Your efforts must match your ambitions. How far do you think you'll have to go to accomplish all your dreams and ambitions when 1000 other people want the same goals as you?

The reality of time is that there are 168 hours in each week. If you work 40 hours a week and sleep eight hours a day, you have 72 hours remaining. If you work out an hour a day, 5 days a week, you are down to 67 hours. Let's toss 14 hours a week of family time or two hours a day, and you now have 53 hours remaining. Throw in some commuting time to and from work, the gym, grocery shopping or other ancillary activities for another 13 hours per week (that's a lot by the way); you still have 40 hours a week to do what you need to do to accomplish the goals you set for yourself. That's an entire second work week! Not to mention you can chip away a few hours of sleep a day if you need to. Six hours is enough for anyone and would add another 14 hours a week. The question isn't whether you have time, it's a matter of what you value and how you spend it.

The real question is, once you've made a proper and honest assessment of your aspirations in comparison to your willingness to hustle, how can you ensure your desire to work hard never fades? How do some people grind endlessly in pursuit of what they desire while others throw in the towel after only a few weeks? How do you forge ahead after countless failures, disappointments, and setbacks? How do you obtain the same level of grit and perseverance that a SEAL possesses? The answer to this question is what everyone should be seeking because while it's easy to say you are going to hustle and persevere, it's much harder to see that action through consistently, day in and day out. It's easy to tell someone how important work ethic is. It's something entirely different to maintain that diligence consistently and indefinitely when nothing but roadblocks and failure seem to line a person's path.

This wall that most people hit is called the "Valley of Despair" and is the third phase in what is known as "The Emotional Cycle of Change." In the 1970s Psychologists Don Kelley and Daryl Connor formulated the original model. This model has been slightly altered over time but remains relatively the same. One of the later models is outlined below.

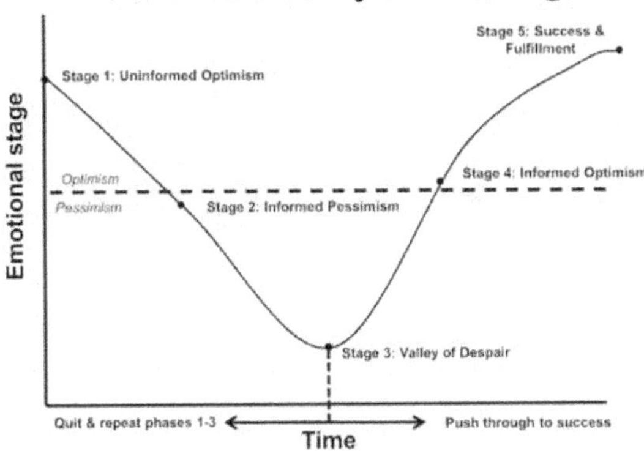

The concept is fairly simple. Anytime we embark on a new adventure of some kind, like starting a new business for example, we deal with the harsh realities of that journey in a series of phases. The first phase is known as "Uninformed Optimism" and basically describes the excitement of starting something new. Maybe you watched a webinar or saw a promo on how to make money drop shipping, or met with your friend about this new business idea over lunch. You were excited, you purchased the starter pack, and you were ready to make a change! But most importantly, the excitement of the new venture overshadowed your understanding of the work it takes to actually become successful at it.

This is where phase two comes in which is called "Informed Pessimism." This is where the harsh reality of the work required to actually succeed kicks in. Very quickly you go from, "Let's do this!" to "Oh man, this is way harder than I thought it was going to be." Your blind optimism becomes pessimism as you begin to realize the long journey that lies ahead of you.

The third phase is what is known as "The Valley of Despair" and is where almost every single person that embarks on something new and difficult quits. This is the wall. This where most say, "I can't do this anymore." It's what the man at the bottom of the picture below is doing.

The fourth phase is "Informed Optimism" which is where you start to see small signs of success that encourage you to keep going. The fifth and final phase is of course success. What ends up happening to most people is that once they hit phase three, they quit, find a shiny new object or goal and start over again in phase one. They then repeat the same process over and over and over again always quitting at phase three, before starting something new, and in turn, never reaching success.

That is why grit is so important. It is the one trait that will propel you through the "Valley of Despair" and toward success. Understanding how to keep that fire going is the holy grail of success. It's just another reason why I believe exercise is so important. The people who do it understand failure, struggle, pain, much more so than those who don't. When you work out, you train your body for resiliency. You train it to endure struggle because you know the payoff exists on the other side.

There are countless examples of this in the real world, and you don't have to look far. J.K. Rowling, for example, the author of one of the most read book series of all time, Harry Potter, was denied 12 times before her first book was picked up by a publisher. Tim Ferriss' first book "The Four-Hour Workweek" was rejected by 27 publishers before it was picked up by Crown Publishing Group in 2007. When Walt Disney pitched his Mickey Mouse idea, it was rejected over 300 times, and before that, he was fired from a newspaper job for "not being creative enough." I was fired from every job I ever had before starting my own company.

What if J.K. Rowling had thrown in the towel after the eighth rejection? What if Walt Disney had scrapped the Mickey Mouse idea after rejection number 204? What if he had taken his boss's comments about not having enough creativity seriously enough to forge a different path?

You need to understand that rejection and failure aren't avoidable. Both, to the contrary, are almost inescapable. The difference between people who find success and those who don't quite often is simply the difference between the two people in the picture above. One person walks away from their dreams, goals, and aspirations when adversity strikes, and the other pursues it endlessly until they achieve what they desire.

Operating Without Fear

The next question then becomes: If grit is a prerequisite of someone's ability to hustle and therefore achieve success, how does one develop the grit, perseverance, and determination required to do so undeterred amongst hardship and failure? The short answer is that you must adopt a state of fearlessness. Now, this doesn't mean that you fear nothing. What it means is that you must operate without the fear of critics or judgment.

To have grit, you must have a willingness to fail. The only way you will ever be able to push aside failure, loss, and criticism repeatedly is if they do not affect you. If the idea that people may judge you if you lose bothers you, it will affect your willingness to take chances. It will weaken your desire to continue and try a second time. If you fear the act of failure or the criticism you could face for failing, it will suffocate your chances for success.

My willingness to fail comes from my fear of regret. I remember being scared out of my mind when I was getting ready to launch my first business. I had saved up a couple hundred thousand dollars over about 5 years, and I was battling with the idea that I could lose all of it. This fear consumed me for about six months as I contemplated leaping. What if I lost everything? What would people say? These were the thoughts racing through my mind almost every day. Every day until "the" day.

I remember driving home one day after constantly wavering on when I was going to leap. I kept putting it off because I was nervous about the repercussions if I failed. Then on that fateful day, as I drove home, it hit me like a ton of bricks. Or rather, the fear left me. Every ounce of fear I had been holding onto about all the potential consequences of failure suddenly left.

The irony is that there was nothing special about this day or the drive home. No event occurred that forever changed my life or anything like that. Nothing happened out of the norm, but for some reason, that drive home has been seared into my memory. I was simply driving home in traffic, and the fear that had consumed me for months seemed to vanish suddenly. It was not because I was suddenly so confident that I would succeed, but because I would never be able to forgive myself if I didn't at least make an attempt.

For me, that was it. It was that simple. For me, it was the absolute realization that my fear of regret was far more overwhelming than my fear of failure. It was more powerful than any fear of criticism from others or any amount of money I could potentially lose. Your catalyst may be different than mine, but you must find it because otherwise, fear will control you. You see, the difference between those who make the leap and who are more likely to succeed aren't the ones who aren't fearful, but the ones who don't allow the fear to dictate their decisions.

You will always quit long before you have the chance to succeed if you worry about what critics are saying or the potential consequences of losing. If you allow things like your parents' potential disappointment in your career choice to affect your decisions; if you worry about what your friends will say after you fail for the third time, or if you allow rumblings of gossip from neighbors or coworkers about your failures, dissuade you from continuing on your path, you will always come up short. The chance of success on your first attempt at anything is almost zero.

This means to have any real chance of success; you must first fail repeatedly before you ever experience success. This continued failure process is what stops most people. They become discouraged, or more importantly, embarrassed because of the opinions of others. They are afraid of their parent's opinions and the views of their friends. In a society where social media rules everything, where every one of our actions and the results of those actions is documented, it is more important than ever to be undeterred by the opinions of others. The only way you will ever succeed or have the will to pursue dreams that others would deem unattainable is if you are first and foremost fearless of failure and the opinions of others. Unfortunately, this is not a quality you can just wake up one day and convince yourself of. The ability to operate without fear only comes to those who are never satisfied.

Never Be Satisfied

Some might think the idea of never being satisfied is equivalent to greed or a continuous lust for more. Some might liken it to being unappreciative of what a person has or has not accomplished. In reality, however, the mindset of never being satisfied is simply one that leads you to understand that no matter how good you are, and no matter how much you have achieved, you can improve and do better. This mentality is seen in the weightlifter who can bench-press 300 pounds – but who has his sights set on 315. It's seen in the musician who has 5 platinum albums but won't rest until he or she wins a Grammy. It's what drives the 11-time all-star to continue being the one who shows up first to practice and leaves last or work tirelessly and endlessly for six championship rings when he already has 5. It's the difference between the 90% of the participants who throw in the towel during SEAL training and the 10% who stay the course. But there is one other key ingredient in all of this.

No Plan B

Let's take a look at this picture one more time because what I am about to say, may just be even more important than anything else with regards to grit. Yes, having a strong sense of self awareness, self-esteem, and humility as we will talk about next chapter can help a lot in developing grit, but what may be even more important is the lack of alternative options.

Take a look at the picture above and tell me that you wouldn't be more motivated and likely to continue if you had NO other options. Imagine your ONLY chance for success was to continue. Or better yet that your ONLY chance for survival was to continue. If you had no plan B, nothing to fall back on, you would be exponentially more likely to continue on.

But if you could walk away, and still go back to a cushy job with a 401k, or back to your parents' house, you just might throw in the towel. This is why I always urge people to throw out the Plan Bs. Plan Bs are where the Plan A dreams go to die.

To be honest it's why some of the toughest and grittiest people in the world are the ones who grew up in the harshest environments. Not only have they been constantly exposed to failure and disappointment to the point where it no longer bothers them, but they will fight harder than anyone because they have NOTH-ING TO LOSE. While you may not be able to control your past or the things that shaped you, you most definitely can eliminate Plan Bs when you lay out your plan for success. Remove options, and grit will naturally come because you will have no other option but to continue.

Chapter Six: The Greatest Lie Ever Told

- Screw passion, do what you're good at -

Grit may be what allows you to withstand failure after failure and continue undeterred in an endless pursuit of your goals. But when does grit and perseverance become delusion? When does the determined pursuit of your passion become a misguided and misinterpreted false sense of reality? When does grit, which I hold in such high regard, become a weakness? When does it become a wolf in sheep's clothing? It happens when you apply blind perseverance and determination without self-awareness.

If success were as simple as unbridled determination, then everyone who works hard would be successful. Unfortunately, that just isn't the case. Grit and determination in and of themselves are not enough to produce success. Hard work alone will have you grasping at straws until the end of time. If hard work alone led to unlimited success construction workers and day laborers would be the richest humans on the planet. That's not the case. Systems, knowledge, experience, expertise, sales ability, people skills, and a myriad of other skillsets are all critical to your success.

Your ability to understand what you excel at and what you don't, so that you can take the necessary steps to gain knowledge in the areas where you are weak is probably the most important thing leading to or standing in the way of your success. Anyone who lacks self-awareness will have their state of fearlessness and grit cloaked in misinterpretation and delusion. Possessing determination is an absolute necessity but having it without self-awareness is just delusion disguised as perseverance.

If you are trying to start a business, you should be asking yourself if you are good at sales. Do you have leadership skills? Do you understand how to create systems and culture? Are you good with technology, social media, etc.? Or, like most people, are you good at some of those things and not others?

The same applies to parents, or if you work in a company and are looking to move up. What skillsets are required of that position and what are you potentially missing? What skillsets do you have that your partner lacks and vice versa for raising children? Hopefully, you balance one another, and each of you fills holes that the other is lacking. That is what makes relationships work, and what makes companies work.

The same is true across the board. The differentiating factor is whether you can truly understand what you are good at and what you lack. Knowing when to work or train a skillset to get it up to par, or when to look for someone else to fill that void is what separates those who win from those who continually try and fail.

The line between determination and delusion is so easily blurred because the two are closely related. Both involve the willingness to endure continued loss and struggle to succeed, but if you lack the necessary discipline to self-evaluate, it is easy for a person to misinterpret one for the other. There is a big difference between someone who is self-aware of their strengths and weaknesses, who pursues a goal or an endeavor with a strong sense of resiliency, and someone who is unaware of them, who pursues a goal in that same manner.

One will understand when it is time to throw in the towel, redirect their energy elsewhere, or potentially bring in someone else who's strengths complement their weaknesses. The other will continue forward, never knowing why success continues to elude them. They will continue to take loss after loss, never being able to critically and objectively analyze themselves or the reasons they are failing.

The Problem isn't Lack of Skill. It's Lack of Recognition of Lack of Skill

I can't tell you how many people I have seen across different industries who just aren't good at what they do, period. They lack the necessary skill set to be good in their industries, and yet they have no clue as to why success eludes them. Instead, they blame it on the economy or their competitors. They blame it on bad luck. They blame it on everything and everyone but themselves because they lack self-awareness and accountability.

I see it in my industry all the time, and it's why I created Gym Rev. A lot of trainers in the fitness industry think just because they are good at training people, they can transition and open a gym or studio. Nothing could be further from the truth. Most trainers are quite horrible at sales; in fact most hate it. They don't understand systems, quality control, or how to extrapolate and interpret KPIs (key performance indicators, such as customer acquisition cost, margins, and others). They don't understand marketing and branding.

Their lack of knowledge in those areas isn't the problem. The problem is the lack of recognition of those deficiencies. It's that they think they can succeed simply by being a good trainer, and they overinflate their abilities in those weak areas. The best thing an owner of any company in any industry can do is have the realization that they need help. As I said in an earlier chapter, it's ok to suck at stuff. We all suck at something.

What's crippling is when we live in denial of what we suck at, or we try to brush it under the table, hoping it won't be an issue. I can promise you that it will always be. Remember that great owners or CEOs aren't great at everything, they are great at building a team that has people that COLLECTIVELY are great at everything.

Self-awareness is one of the first qualities I look for when hiring someone. Without it, how can you ever expect to fix shortcomings and bad habits, or leverage the things you are good at? We are all born with innate gifts upon which we can build our success. For a select few, passion and talent are one. However, for 90% of the population, the two don't always align perfectly. What someone believes to be their passion can be vastly different than the skillsets and talents they possess. Your passion may be basketball, and your dream may be to play in the NBA, but if you're 35 and still playing in amateur leagues trying to make it to the show, you seriously need to re-evaluate where your skills lie.

There's nothing inherently wrong with chasing your passion, and I am not here to crush your dreams of entering the NFL draft or becoming the next hip-hop icon. What I am here to do is to ensure you uncover the path with the greatest chance for your success. Remember that your passion for basketball can be fulfilled by doing something else in the industry outside of playing the sport itself. You can still fulfill passion while simultaneously leveraging the things you are good at. We all know the person who has the worst voice anyone has ever heard and still goes on American Idol to audition because their mom told them they were a great singer. Don't be that person.

The Greatest Lie Ever Told

"Pursue your passion," is what they tell you. "That's the only way you'll ever be successful." I call bullsh*t. It's a lie. In fact, I believe it's the greatest lie ever told. Don't pursue passion. Instead, pursue the thing you excel in. "Pursue your passion" is a fraud. Success comes from skill set, not passion.

The amazing thing about pursuing skill over passion though is that when you follow that which you are good at and you will eventually uncover passions you probably never even knew you had. It's human nature to find pleasure in the things we are good at. It's in our DNA to find gratification in things we receive positive reinforcement from. We enjoy doing things we excel at for that very reason. When you double-down and pursue your skill sets passion and skill become one.

This is why it is so important to experiment and try different things. Not only will it help you discover what you enjoy, but it will also uncover what you were meant to do. Most people don't know what they are good at until they stumble upon it. The problem is that most people never take the time to search for it, and because of that, most of the population NEVER realize their true talents.

I, for one, never knew I had a passion for business until I fell into it. I didn't know what my passion was or what I wanted to do, even after five years of college. Yes, five. If not for some twist of fate, I would have never found my true passion. Often, we pursue the interests we are surrounded by. It's the reason so many kids whose parents are police officers or firefighters tend to follow the same footsteps. It's why there are multiple generations of so many professions. Your experiences, more often than not, will be the things you'll be pulled toward doing yourself. That doesn't necessarily mean that it is what you should be doing, though.

I fell into that same category. My father and uncle were both in law enforcement. After college and still not knowing what I wanted to follow as a career, I found myself applying to the LAPD. Not because that was what I was passionate about, but because that was what I knew. Don't get me wrong; law enforcement is one of the most honorable and undervalued professions in the world. I have more respect for what they do than probably anyone, but just because I respect it doesn't mean that it was what I was born to do. It means I was about to pursue a career that "made sense" at the time. The irony of this entire story, however, is that the LAPD rejected me because of numerous poor decisions I had made growing up.

Only after being turned away was I able to venture into other industries and explore other options. This is how I found my passion and talent for business and people. Failing and getting turned away in one profession is what ultimately led me to my current success. If I hadn't been rejected by LAPD, I might have never discovered what I was incredibly good at.

I tell this story in hopes that you learn from my mistakes. I tell this story because not everyone will get a second chance to discover what they are good at. Had I been accepted into the police department, I would not have written this book. More importantly, I never would have discovered my true passion. It's not to say that I wouldn't have loved being a cop, but I know that my talents are better used for what I do now. So, when you look at the path you are about to take, just make sure that you never pursue something because it "makes sense" at the time.

Never pursue something simply because it's "all you know." The only way you will ever find out what you are genuinely good at is if you follow your own path. If you are good at and have a passion for video games, but your parents want you to become a college professor because it is what they did, remember that it's your life and your dream, not theirs. Understand your skillsets and follow that. You are not here to follow the same path everyone else does; you are here to make your own. Don't wait for the world to force your hand as I did. Not everyone gets a second chance or ends up as fortunate.

Self-esteem Doesn't Come From You; It Comes From Others

This is a message to all parents about the importance of building your child's self-esteem early on. Encourage them and praise them, but never lie to them. Support them in trying different things so that they can discover what they are good at but hold them accountable in finishing whatever they start. And most of all, allow them to lose. No matter how much it hurts to see your loved ones lose, it is what will teach them how to pick themselves back up. If you fail at teaching them how to lose early in life when consequences are less severe, when they lose later in life, they will quit. Remember that the only reason people like Walt Disney, J.K. Rowling, or even someone like me were ever able to continue to push through failure or rejection is that we lost early and often in life. And when you are exposed to loss, you realize it's not all that bad. If anything, it just helps you gain perspective and confidence.

It's no coincidence that self-esteem, and self-awareness have a strong commonality in the word "self." However, the irony is that neither have anything to do with self-imposed critiques or accolades, but instead with the critiques and accolades you receive from everyone else. Understanding this is crucial to being able to overcome whatever self-doubts you may have.

Every ounce of self-esteem you have comes from outside opinions and feedback. Our entire picture of self-worth and value is based purely on our interpretation of other people's opinions we receive daily. No one starts day one thinking they suck. It's only after they are told they suck that they begin to question whether it's true or not. At the same time, when we are given accolades for something, we begin to build higher self-worth. The importance of understanding that self-esteem is primarily derived from other people's opinions cannot be understated.

Generally speaking, you are going to receive three types of feedback for anything and everything you do. Positive, negative, and neutral. On the surface, that might seem simple enough. You'd think that if you do something well, you will receive positive feedback, and if you do something poorly, you will receive negative feedback, and anything in between would be neutral. However, it's not quite that simple because there are a couple of variations of each type. Not all positive feedback is good, not all negative feedback is bad, and not all neutral reactions are neutral. The devil is in the detail.

For positive feedback, there exists what I like to call "true positives" and "false positives." Feedback that is a "true positive" is an encouragement given for something that deserves it. Something as simple as rewarding a child for getting straight As in school or holding the door open for a stranger are both examples of good variations of positive feedback.

The not-so-good version is the "false positive" variation. This is where positive feedback or encouragement is given regardless of whether it's deserved. An example might be giving your son the same reward as your daughter even though he got a D in science, and she got an A. This would have the potential for a couple of adverse side effects. One is that it begins to blur the lines between good performance and bad performance, which has a drastic impact on someone's perception of reality. The second issue is that if the same rewards or accolades are given for two entirely different levels of performance, it is human nature to move toward a lesser willingness to succeed since the rewards for winning or losing are relatively the same.

For negative feedback, the two variations are what I like to call "destructive negative feedback" and "constructive negative feedback." The difference being that destructive negative feedback is given without any desire to alter or improve the performance in question, and constructive negative feedback acknowledges the shortcomings but is offered in a way to encourage fixing the problem. This is the difference between a parent taking away their child's phone and telling them they're stupid because they got a D in math vs. the same parent taking away their child's phone for a week while at the same time trying to find ways to help or improve their school work.

In either example, the feedback above acknowledges a deficiency in performance, but how that message is delivered is entirely different. It's the same thing with neutral responses. If good performance is met with neutral responses, it can be just as bad as it is met with a false positive.

So why does all this matter? It matters because good self-esteem doesn't come from positive feedback alone and poor self-esteem from negative feedback. Good self-esteem and self-awareness are created through a combination of positive feedback and constructive negative feedback, and poor self-esteem/awareness is created through a combination of false-positive feedback and or destructive negative feedback.

Not only is this crucial for all parents to understand this, but it's also essential to every person reading this book to understand how important the people we surround ourselves with are. This is the critical link between the second and third pillars of success; grit, and your inner circle. The two pillars which are directly linked to your ability to overcome fear.

You cannot create self-esteem out of thin air. You can, however, put yourself in an environment where the people who affect it are the kind that will add to it rather than break it down. We all suck at something. We all suck at a lot of things. What makes people successful isn't that they suck at nothing; it's that they find and pursue the situations where they excel.

Surrounding yourself with positive, like-minded, driven individuals will encourage you to try things you would never have tried before. They will stand behind you, encourage, and support your ideas and passions. They will hold you accountable when you need a reminder that you can do better. And ultimately, over time, they will give you the confidence to resist allowing other people's opinions to alter your self-worth, which is the only way to operate fearlessly along a path built on skill rather than passion alone.

There are Winners and Losers. Your Participation Trophy Doesn't Change That

If all we ever do is praise someone and never correct or acknowledge faults or shortcomings, that individual will have a sense of confidence that's potentially jaded. Being able to deploy accurate self-awareness properly is the ability to balance positive reinforcement while steering clear of the "participation trophy" culture. Nowadays, we give trophies out to every kid on every team regardless of how well that team or individual does in a given sport. It's as if we are afraid to tell our children they lost.

We put their momentary feelings ahead of what is beneficial to them. There is this rampant misconception that says by awarding trophies to every child regardless of effort or skill; we are somehow instilling this necessary confidence when the truth is we are creating a false reality. It's not only blurring the lines between success and failure, but it's also teaching that failure or loss should be avoided when in reality failure and loss are a part of life and a necessary process that must occur to win and achieve success. Allowing someone to know they failed is the only way someone can ever overcome failure and succeed in the future. It's the only way someone can correct their course.

How is someone supposed to get better without first knowing that they in fact need to get better? It's as if one day we decided that it would be better to lie to our children rather than tell them the truth because the truth might hurt their feelings. We decided rather than teaching our children that losing and failure are a part of life, that we are better off just handing a trophy to all regardless of effort, success, and skillset. By opting to shield our kids from loss and failure in the short term, we damage their understanding of how the world works in the long term.

The truth is that for every winner, there must be at least one loser. And quite often, for every winner, there are dozens or even thousands of losers. That's how real-life works. For every person who gets promoted, dozens don't. For every person who gets hired, hundreds never get a callback. For every person that is accepted to a college or receives a scholarship, thousands are denied. Competition is inherent in our society. Competition is natural; it is what challenges us to become better. To pretend that competition does not exist or to award everyone equally regardless of work ethic, effort, or skill, is to strip us of our primal motivation for success. Understanding that loss and failure are a part of life, and learning to overcome them, is what will lead you down the path of success.

This lesson doesn't stop at our kids either. You might be self-sabotaging your own success by shielding yourself from loss and failure in the same way some parents shield their children from it. The worst thing we can do to our children and ourselves is to blur the line between winning and losing. When we do so, we strip away our inherent desire to perform. If you shield yourself from the potential of losing, you, in turn, shield yourself from discovering what you excel at and what you don't. Self-awareness is an impossibility without engaging in competition with the potential for loss. Competition is your placeholder in life. To shy away from it because of a fear of failure or loss will destroy your ability to become self-aware.

To ignore the fact that there are winners and losers is to live in denial. Competition exists in everything we do, and to have a real chance at success, you must have an inherent desire to win or be the best. Competition is innate. It's a part of what makes us human. Having a threat of loss incentivizes performance, drives competition, and ignites ambition. If you take away your understanding of loss, you remove your drive for victory.

I always attempt to surround myself with people who are successful, positive, and who, most of all, challenge me to be better. If anything, I want to surround myself with people who are MORE successful than I am. I use the same philosophy when working out. I always seek to work out with people who are stronger or in better shape than I am because it pushes me—surrounding yourself with people that are better than you forces you to improve. It forces you to become stronger and more resilient. Never surround yourself with people who make you feel comfortable. Surround yourself with people that will push you outside of your comfort zone. Surround yourself with people that will continuously and forever push you to be a better version of yourself every day.

Start Working Out. Not Next Week, Not Tomorrow: Now.

Fitness has always been a huge part of my entire life. Not because I grew up working out and playing sports or because it's the industry in which I do business but exercising and eating healthy gives me a strong sense of confidence day in and day out. It gives me the energy needed to power through long days at work. I consider myself a high-energy individual, and fitness gives me the fuel I need to keep that energy throughout the day. If you don't already work out, you need to start tomorrow. Not next week, not in a month, tomorrow. I promise you that it will improve your life in every way imaginable.

It will give you the energy and confidence to deal with whatever the world throws your way. It will enhance the way you raise your children, how you interact with friends and coworkers, the way you carry yourself, the way you speak in public, and the confidence you exude when you shake someone's hand. Working out will change your body, but more importantly, it will change your mindset, and changing your mindset will change your life.

Courage in Humility

Humility is the catalyst for moving into a state of fearlessness because humility is OK with failure. Humility is OK with loss. You have to understand how huge this is. When I talk about humility, I am not refencing it in terms of being humble. I am referencing humility as it relates to your willingness to fail.

Humility is what enables you to take the leap in the first place. Not only that, but humility is what grants you the ability to ask for help when you need it most. It would be incredibly arrogant for any successful person to claim they got to where they were without the help of others. I created a dedication in this book specifically for that reason. I understand just as you should that behind every great athlete are the coaches, trainers, friends, and family who supported, encouraged, taught, and enabled the athlete to excel.

Behind every successful entrepreneur are a set of staff, investors, mentors, friends, and family who encouraged, supported, believed in, and pushed the entrepreneur. Behind every great parent are the parents before them, their family, and their friends. Behind every successful individual are groups of people who helped mold and shape that individual. Acknowledging those individuals is one of the primary keys to success but acknowledging that it's okay to seek help in the first place is what truly makes the difference.

It's funny to me how many things in life parallel working out. Everyone knows they should workout, but so many people never do. Not because they don't know it's good for them, but because a lot of people just don't like to. It's hard, it takes work, and the results are far from instantaneous. The journey to success is similar. It's never pretty, it's not always fun, and it often requires time and sacrifices that you just don't want to make. But much like working out, something miraculous happens a few months in if you can just push through. You start to see some results.

Maybe it's just the lighting in the mirror that morning, but it doesn't matter because it feels good. It feels rewarding. You start to think to yourself; maybe this pain is worth it after all. Maybe getting up when your alarm went off at 5 AM every day is paying off. And so, you head to the gym with a little more energy the next day. You do it again the next day, and again the day after that. Pretty soon, it becomes second nature, and you almost find yourself enjoying it.

That's what happens when you push through those first few months of discomfort. This doesn't just happen with working out either. It happens when you begin to see any kind of success begin to form. That's what happens when discipline forms. That's how grit is forged and how success is bred. It changes your mindset, the way you think, how you act, and it expands on what you believe is possible. It changes your priorities and your focus. Grit is one of the most significant predictors of success, and this is the path to executing it.

There is one more ingredient that you must have though or everything I have just talked about will have been a waste. You need to optimize your chances of following through on your plan and the only way to do that is to create an environment that encourages all of these things. To ever have the courage to throw out your Plan B, to have the self-awareness to pursue your talents over passions, or to develop the necessary grit to attack all of it fearlessly, your environment must be primed to do so. There's only one way to do this, and that's to get rid of your loser friends.

Chapter Seven: Get Rid of Your Loser Friends

"If you look at your inner circle and you aren't inspired, you don't have a circle, you have a cage."-Nipsy Hustle (1985-2019)

"It's not what you know, but who you know." This is a statement we've all heard a thousand times, but the question is whether there's any truth behind it. Does the idea that relationships are more important than knowledge hold any weight? Think about it, if I were able to grant you one wish, and you could either choose all the knowledge in the world or the ability to know and have a relationship with anyone and everyone in the world, which would you choose?

It's pretty much a win-win scenario as both have tremendous upside potential, but I would argue that most people would take limitless knowledge. I mean, why wouldn't you? There would be nothing you wouldn't know. You would have the answer to literally everything, and success would be a foregone conclusion.

So why then, if knowledge has so much power, does the saying, "It's not what you know, but who you know" have so much weight in our society? Why do so many people live and die by that concept? Why is your inner circle one of the Seven Pillars of Success? I'll tell you why, but it's probably not for the reason you would think.

Most people understand the phrase as describing the importance of shaking hands and meeting influential people so you can leverage relationships for jobs, networking, etc. It's the idea that while one person may be extremely qualified for a job, a person less qualified may land the position because they know the owner or the person in charge of hiring. If you're in sales and trying to land a huge account, having a relationship with one or more decision-makers in the company will significantly increase your chances of closing the sale. It's because you are human, and humans like doing business with people we know and like.

Who you know, and more importantly, whom you surround yourself with, has an uncompromising impact on every skillset and personality trait you possess. The people in your inner circle will affect your confidence, perspective, positivity, and ambition to execute. The people you surround yourself with will either aid in your success or cripple it. Trust me when I tell you that your inner circle is the unwavering foundation for grit and everything that comes before it.

You'll notice that this is how the Seven Pillars of Success work within each of the four phases. The pillars of success work cohesively with one another. For them to work effectively, they must all be present because they are meant to work together. Here in phase two, grit may be the trait most closely linked to success, but the pillar of success that creates the environment that enables it in the first place is your inner circle.

Who You Know is Knowledge and Knowledge is Power

Who you know is vital for things like networking because, as you've already learned by reading this book, relationships are king. However, who you know is also important because it can drastically affect what you know and the environment in which you operate. It can positively or negatively affect who you are as a person. Who you know not only gives you an edge when it comes to leveraging relationships but when you surround yourself with people who are smarter than you, more successful than you, more connected than you, you learn.

When you surround yourself with positive and energetic people who challenge you, I promise that what you will not only increase your networking ability; it will change who you are as a person. Surround yourself with the right people, and it will change your environment for the better. Surround yourself with the wrong people, however, and it will be the most detrimental thing you can do to your success. It's time to get rid of your loser friends. Changing your inner circle does three main things. It acts as the support structure of grit, it allows you to leverage the simple fact that people like to do business with people they know, and finally, it increases your knowledge base and skillset. Let's dive into the latter two now.

One of the benefits of having a well-connected inner circle is the ability to create more opportunities. When you are well connected, it is just a simple and straightforward fact that more doors will open. But let's be honest, who you know just gets you in the door. You may know and have great relationships with a ton of people, but if you lack skill, if you lack knowledge, if you lack discipline or talent, how far you will go will be limited. Increase your knowledge and your skillset, however, and you will find that doors will soon begin to open themselves. The real secret behind the phrase, "It's not what you know, but who you know" isn't in its ability to open doors for you; it's in its ability to leverage relationships for knowledge. It's important not that you know a fisherman so that you can eat, but so he can teach you how to fish.

A high school friend of mine is the head chef for a winery in Paso Robles, CA, and part owner in Locally Grown, a catering company based in the LA area. What's impressive isn't that he's become a successful chef and business owner, but how he got to that point that's noteworthy. His rise to success wasn't by fluke; it wasn't by luck. His success was a well-executed game plan. He understood the value of surrounding himself with people who knew more and were more experienced than he was. He realized that it's about who you know. He knew the value of surrounding himself not just with people better than himself, but also surrounding himself with people who were the best in the industry.

Knowing the importance of your inner circle is one thing. Going out and changing it is an entirely different ballgame, especially when you lack a relationship in the industry you are looking to get involved in. This was the situation my friend was in. He lacked established relationships with any of the top chefs or restaurants in the world. Shoot, he didn't even have a relationship with a mediocre industry professional. He knew relationships were necessary; he just didn't have any. So, how then was he supposed to leverage relationships he didn't have? Easy. He forced his way in.

You see, most people fail to win because they fail to execute, and they fail to execute because they make excuses. They'll make excuses like, "I don't know anyone" or "It's not fair because so-and-so has better connections than I do." They look for an excuse rather than a solution. The mindset that separates those two ways of thinking is the difference between winning and losing. Excuses are made by people who are destined to fail. Solutions, no matter how bleak, are what winners focus on.

My friend could easily have said, "I don't have any connections with the best chefs or restaurateurs in the world," and just tried to do it on his own. He could have made a list of excuses, but instead he looked for a solution. He decided that if there wasn't a relationship to open a door for him, that he'd open it himself.

So, he picked up the phone. He got on the internet. He got on Facebook, Instagram, and Twitter. He used every available resource he could, and he started calling, messaging, and emailing every world-renowned chef and restaurateur he could find. When he was finally able to get a hold of someone, he didn't ask for a job. He didn't ask for help or assistance. He told them that wherever they were, he would fly out and sleep on the floor of a run-down apartment if necessary, so that he could work for them for free. He told them that he would do whatever they needed. He would scrub the floors, he would run errands, help in the kitchen, he would do anything and everything they would ask of him in exchange for one thing; to learn from the best.

He was rejected again and again, probably because the restaurant owners and chefs thought he was joking. They probably thought he was crazy. Undeterred, he kept calling until finally, his efforts paid off. One of the most famous chefs in the world from Chicago took him in. He immediately flew out, and for six months worked for free and learned from the best in the world. He cleaned the floors, waited tables, helped in the kitchen, and ran errands.

He did anything and everything asked of him, and in his spare time, he watched and asked questions. He assisted with cooking and preparing. He learned. He learned more in six months than he could ever have learned in four years at school. He did it because he understood that who you know is important because of what you can learn from them.

Think about it, what if you could learn and study under the most celebrated entrepreneur, chef, attorney, sports agent, or the best in whatever industry you are passionate about. Would you? Consider how much you could learn. Think about how much free work you could leverage for an endless amount of knowledge. Not only would you be able to build and leverage future relationships, but you could potentially increase your knowledge base exponentially as well.

Surrounding yourself with people that are better, smarter, and more experienced than you will be more valuable than anything else you could ever do. I would argue that spending six months interning directly under someone like Grant Cardone, Jeff Bezos, Elon Musk, Gary Vaynerchuck, a top-level music or movie producer, or anyone at the top of their industry, is 100x more valuable than any four or eight year education you can get at a university.

Here's the kicker, though. The impact of who you surround yourself with doesn't just stop at the opportunities it creates or the knowledge and skillsets you can acquire. Quite possibly, the most impactful thing it can do for your success is that it can change your mindset and how effectively and diligently you pursue your goals. Think about it.

If you were able to surround yourself with people that are smarter than you, more driven than you, more detail-oriented and organized, exuded more confidence, were willing to take risks, and had better energy than you, do you think you would start to pick up on some of those traits and skillsets? Don't you think you would adopt some of those same tendencies? I am telling you without a shadow of a doubt you would. Just remember, though, that just as easily as you would start to adopt beneficial skillsets, you have the same ability to adopt poor habits and skillsets over time by surrounding yourself with lazy or negative individuals.

We Adapt to the Tribe Around Us

This isn't just a theory; it's ingrained in our biology. Study after study has proven that we as humans, have an innate desire to be a part of a collective group. History has also shown that we have an uncanny ability to adapt to our surroundings. These two undeniable truths mean that we not only have a desire to be a part of a larger tribe, but we are willing to adapt and conform to make it happen. It's part of what makes us human, and it's a part of what has allowed us to survive as a species for thousands of years.

What this means for you is that you will, over time, mold to your surroundings whether you want to or not. It isn't something you have a choice over; it's in your DNA. So instead of fighting it, let's leverage it instead. Our ability and desire to adapt to our surroundings began as a survival instinct. Now it's time to use it to your advantage not just to survive but to thrive. It's time to leverage your surroundings and the people around you so that when you adapt, you adapt upward and not downward.

So then the question becomes if you understand how impactful a mentor can be, and you understand how easily we as a species conform to our surroundings, how can you not also understand that the people you immediately surround yourself with; your friends, coworkers, business partners, and family, can have the exact same impact on your future? It's time that you start to audit who you surround yourself with, because not only can they impact your knowledge base, but the people you surround yourself with will, 100 percent, impact your success.

The unfortunate aspect is that most people's surroundings aren't geared for success, and so they simply fall into the same rat race as their friends and coworkers. It's human nature. Surely you've heard the saying that success breeds success. However, this concept holds true for anything. Mediocrity breeds mediocrity. Complacency breeds complacency. Negativity breeds negativity. You see, whatever environment you are in will slowly and subconsciously mold you in the same way.

If Your Significant Other is Holding You Back, Get Rid of Them

The catalyst to accomplish all that you set out will be the five people you spend the most time with. That's it—five. And yes, that includes your significant other so if they are not creating an abundance of positivity and support in your life and all your endeavors, then you need to remove them from your life. And no, I am not joking.

These five people are the ones who are subconsciously affecting your thoughts and actions, and it is your responsibility to remove those who are holding you back. This can and should begin with your spouse or significant other. I know this isn't an easy topic to broach, nor do I expect it to be something that will be easy to execute. If after you do the upcoming analysis on whether your closest five should be removed from your inner circle, and your spouse doesn't make the cut, you will need to do some serious soul searching.

I have been blessed with an amazing wife who supports me in anything and everything I do. Trust me when I say that I firmly believe I would not have had the level of success I've reached without her. The term power couple exists for a reason, primarily because they make each other better. My wife challenges me, she supports me, she has a positivity, genuineness, and energy about her that draws you in.

She gives me perspective when managing my companies in ways that I wouldn't always think of alone. She does all these things and a hundred more that I don't have time to list, but this is what your spouse should do for you. Remember, you only have space for five people in your inner circle, and your spouse automatically takes up one of those crucial five slots, so you had better make it count, because after that you only have four slots left.

Your life will be full of circumstances you can't control. It's why it is so important to take ownership of the things you can. Think about it like this; If one person's four closest friends were four of the most successful people on the planet, and another person's four closest friends were jobless and unmotivated, whom do you think would be better prepared for success?

At the beginning of chapter four, I proposed you ask yourself a question. Who do you need to become to accomplish your dreams? Now I pose a second question.

Who Must You Surround Yourself With to Create the Person You Need to Become?

There is no secret formula for determining which of your friends you should distance yourself from, but the irony is you probably already know who should be removed from your inner circle you just need to follow your gut.

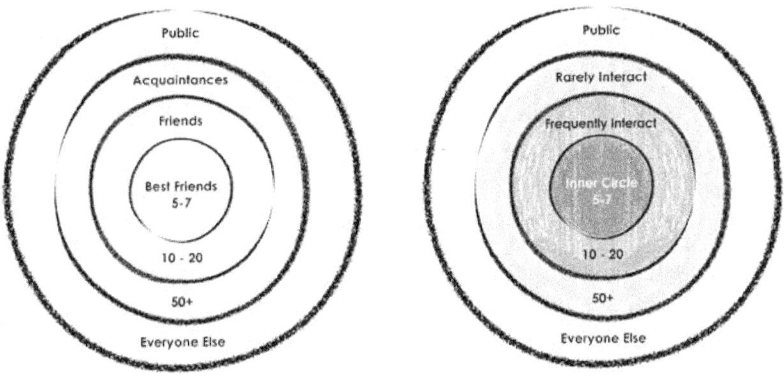

What you are going to do first is, using the above diagram, place each of your friends, coworkers, and anyone else you spend a decent amount of time with into one of those categories. Each person can only be in one level of the circle, and you cannot exceed the maximum number listed for any group, so think carefully. Remember, your inner circle can only have five people in it, so include your significant other if you have one, and then the other four people you spend those most time with.

This brings me to the second part of the exercise. You may be noticing there are two circle diagrams. One shows the correct way to assess your inner circle, and the other shows the incorrect way most people do it. In a proper assessment, you don't get to "choose" where people go. You need to base this on time spent with people, not on how good a friend they are. The circle diagram that has "best friends" in the middle is wrong.

The real way to do this properly is the diagram with the "inner circle" in the middle. This is critical because what most people do incorrectly here is put their significant other and four best friends in the inner circle category, which is wrong. Your inner circle MUST be the five people you SPEND THE MOST TIME WITH. The trigger for this exercise is TIME.

After you have correctly assessed which four people (in addition to your significant other) you SPEND THE MOST TIME WITH (not including children of course), you then move on to the next level of time spent—place between 10-20 people in that category. Now, you can do the same thing for the 50 plus category, but, honestly, it's not necessary. What matters most are the first two circles, with the center circle being the primary focus of this exercise. Once you have identified the 5 people, you spend the most time with and the 10-20 people you spend the next most substantial amount of time with, you can move on to the next step. Remember to rank these people based on time spent, NOT level of friendship.

The next step is to look at what skillsets or traits these people possess. How successful are they? Do they exhibit things like positivity and confidence or are they negative and lazy? What are their ambitions? This is usually where the experience becomes eye-opening as most people find out that the individuals they spend the most time with don't just lack humility but are entitled. These are the people who don't just lack ambition but are also lazy. These are the types of people you should remove entirely from your life. These are people who won't just slow you down but will cripple you. Identify these people and make sure that they get pushed to the outer edges of the diagram.

If these individuals aren't outright bad influences then they are likely "neutral." What this means is they are essentially good people with good intentions, but lack traits such as discipline, ambition, desire, etc. This is likely where the bulk of your friends, family, and coworkers will lie. These are the ones that aren't necessarily holding you back, but also aren't pushing themselves or you forward.

They aren't necessarily lazy, but they aren't driven either. They aren't negative, but they aren't enthusiastic. They are merely complacent. You don't need to get rid of these people entirely, but they should be removed from your inner circle and pushed to the second layer of the diagram. They aren't bad people but just are on a different path or trajectory than you desire to be.

The point of this exercise, however, isn't just to rank and remove your current circle, it's to CREATE a POWERFUL inner five. So by the end of this exercise you should aim for your inner circle of five people to characterize the following:

One Pillar of Support: Typically, this is your significant other assuming they possess all the qualities one should look for, but it doesn't have to be. What matters more than their title represents that through good times and bad, they are always there for you.

One Mentor: Someone who has accomplished the things you want to achieve, who has experienced failures and challenges and has come out on the other side.

Two Journeymen: Two others who are climbing with you. Not in the same business, but who have the same ambition and drive. A journey to the top can be lonely. It helps when you have people on the same path.

One Builder/Connector: It's time to start leveraging relationships. Who is the person who can help you open doors? This is the chef my friend sought out. You can trade your time for their expertise, knowledge, and connections. If you want to improve your inner circle, this is where you level it up. Seek them out.

I'm setting a goal for you right now to remove one loser friend from your circle by the end of the week and replace him or her with someone who is going to make you better. By the end of the month, I want you to have removed and replaced two. By the end of three months, I want you to have surrounded yourself with only people who push you to be better, who challenge you, who embody everything we have discussed over the last few chapters. More than anything else, this is how you put everything into motion.

Environment Over Willpower

Your inner circle is the most critical component in Phase 2 as they are what will provide you with the strength to persevere when things get tough. Let's be real, willpower is great, but it will never trump environment. If you're a recovered alcoholic you can have the greatest willpower in the world, but the chances of you remaining sober drops to almost zero if all you do is hang out with people that still drink every day. The same thing goes for hanging out with losers or lazy people if you are trying to be successful. This is environment over willpower. Remember this:

> *If your four closest friends are criminals, you'll be the fifth.*
> *If your four closest friends are negative, pessimistic, and lazy, you'll be the fifth.*
> *If you four closest friends are wealthy and successful, you'll be the fifth.*
> *Get rid of your loser friends.*

PHASE 3: F**K REGRET

Chapter Eight: Passing on One Marshmallow Now for Two Later

-The Power of Delayed Gratification-

If there's one thing I believe I have a gift for, it's working with people. I've always had an innate ability to understand what makes people tick, what motivates them, and what drives them to do the things they do. I study people, analyze decisions and behavior, and I believe it's that innate gift to understand what drives people's actions that led me to become a good leader.

Learning to understand how a person's beliefs, along with emotions like fear, regret, passion, and love, can impact someone's decisions has allowed me to understand behavior and, ultimately, business. Welcome to Phase 3: F**k Regret. Not only will we dive headfirst into how to leverage the powerful emotion of regret, but we will weave together two pillars of success to create your defense mechanism for it — delayed gratification and deadlines.

Great leaders inspire others to action. They lead by example. They lead through purpose and not by desired results. A true leader knows how to balance enthusiasm with discipline. A great leader knows when to implement accountability and when to show empathy. These are the things I live by to extract the absolute best out of my entire team every single day. The amazing part is, my understanding of human behavior hasn't just helped me to develop my employees or my businesses but I have also used it to develop and improve myself. I analyze myself in the same manner.

I constantly audit my actions, my decisions, how I engage with others, and how effective those interactions are. I am always learning, developing, and aiming to become better every day. This understanding of human behavior isn't relegated to being useful for just leaders of companies so they can leverage employees. As I just said, I use these same tactics to leverage my actions and decisions daily so that I stay focused and driven. You can use these same strategies to take advantage of your own actions and behavior. By learning how to leverage your beliefs, passions, and emotions, you, too, can take control of your own life and the way you move through it.

As we discussed earlier, while we like to think of ourselves as logical or rational beings when it comes to the decisions we make, we are far from it. The reality is that our emotions and not rational thought are what drive us. Our beliefs guide us.

This type of thinking is coded into every decision we make. It's the reason we look up to those who inspire us. It's the reason we buy products from companies whose beliefs align with our own. It is why people work for companies whose missions and goals coincide with their beliefs longer than companies that simply pay more. This is hardwired into our DNA. The biggest and most successful companies in the world know this. It's how they sell products effectively. It's why so many ad campaigns are not about the product, but a company's belief as a whole.

So that I can illustrate this fully, let's look at one such company that probably does what we're discussing better than anyone, Nike. Nike has one of the most recognizable slogans that has ever been created. "Just do it." While part of its effectiveness lies in its simplicity, the real reason it is so powerful is that it has nothing at all to do with shoes. It has to do with a mindset. "Just do it" is empowering. In three words, it gives someone purpose. It tells you to challenge the status quo and defy the odds. It screams at you to be better than you were yesterday and to shoot for the stars. It begs you to dream bigger than you have ever dreamed before.

Nike is probably the best in the world at running campaigns that elicit human emotion. It's campaigns like their 2012 "Find your Greatness," or their 2019 "Dream Crazier" commercial. In neither of those campaigns or dozens of others did they sell anything. They didn't pitch a jersey or a shoe. They never once mentioned a sale. Instead, all they did was tap into human emotion. They made you choke up while watching them. They inspired through feelings of triumph and community. Nike doesn't sell shoes; they sell the power of the human spirit. The shoes and apparel they sell are just a symbol of that. You don't buy Nike's because they are made better than any other shoe. You buy them because you believe what Nike believes.

Nike understands how the human brain works, and they use that knowledge to turn you into becoming a life-long customer. The best companies in the world do this. The greatest salespeople in the world do this. We do it at my companies and is why it's engrained into our mission statement at Afterburn Fitness.

We believe:
that fitness isn't just about the destination,
it's about the journey. It's about pursuing passion,
pushing boundaries and defying the odds.
You see, the thing that most often defines our lives,
Is not what happens after we take the first step.
It's whether we take the first step at all.
Remember that we all start somewhere.
Remember that what you are capable of,
is only limited by what you believe is possible.
Remember that no matter who you are,
how old you are, or where your journey begins,
There is an athlete in all of us.

Notice the very first line that says, "We believe." There's a very well thought out purpose for that. It's because emotion and belief systems are what drive behavior. People want to belong and connect with something. They want to be inspired. This emotional response to decision making is illustrated in a well-documented study called "The Marshmallow Test." It's a study that aligns perfectly with the entire concept of this chapter and the fourth pillar of success, Delayed Gratification.

The Marshmallow Test

In the 1960s, a Stanford professor named Walter Mischel began a series of critical studies. Hundreds of children between the ages of four and five were studied and then followed for 40 years. The results were astounding, and much in the same way grit was determined to be one of the most significant predictors of success, the results of this study showed that people who were able to delay gratification held that same title. Here's how the study worked and what was concluded.

The experiment began by bringing each child into a room, sitting them down at a table, and then placing a marshmallow in front of them. The researcher then offered the child a deal. He told the boy or girl that he was going to leave the room and that if the child didn't eat the marshmallow by the time he returned, that he or she would get a second marshmallow. However, if by the time the researcher returned, the child had eaten the first marshmallow, then they would not get a second one. The choice was simple. One treat now or two later.

The researcher left the room for 15 minutes and videotaped the entire process. You can imagine the hilarity that ensued as these children battled with temptation. Some without hesitation scarfed down the marshmallow the second the door closed while others did their best to defy their urges, staring at the marshmallow, squirming in their seats. Most of them fought valiantly but failed. There were, however, a few who were able to stand the test of time and were rewarded with a second marshmallow for doing so.

While this experiment was entertaining and gave a reasonably funny insight into the behavioral patterns of children, the real research came years later. You see, what they did was follow each one of these children for the next 40 years. That's right, 40 years. They conducted follow up interviews, tracked their progress, analyzed their SAT scores, and more. Here's the crazy part. In almost every measurable test performed over the next 40 years, the children who were able to hold out and not eat the marshmallow in those 15 minutes performed better. They had higher SAT scores, lower levels of substance abuse, lower obesity rates, better social skills, and higher incomes.

Their ability to delay gratification didn't stop at the marshmallow. It extended into every decision they ever made, which resulted in greater success in life. Whatever emotional state they were in at 5-years-old that gave them the discipline to opt for delayed gratification over instant gratification propelled them forward in almost every aspect of their lives for the 40 years that followed.

The logical follow-up assumption would be that the ability to delay gratification is just in some people's DNA. Perhaps some people have it, and some don't. And yet, if you thought that, you'd be wrong because a different set of researchers picked up where the original study left off to answer that very question. They wanted to know if this was something that could be learned, or if it was just a skillset that some possessed, and others didn't.

What they found was that the propensity to delay gratification was, in fact, teachable. Not only was it teachable to the ones who weren't able to hold out in the beginning, but they were also able to change the behavior of kids who passed the test the first time around. What this second research group did was take a group of children around the same age as the first study and split them into two groups. They gave the first group a reliable set of experiences. In other words, they would replicate the original scenario by doing something like giving a child a small box of crayons and then offering the child a larger box of crayons if they performed a specific task. Once that task was completed, they would then simply follow through with the promise and provide the child with a larger box of crayons. Pretty straightforward, right?

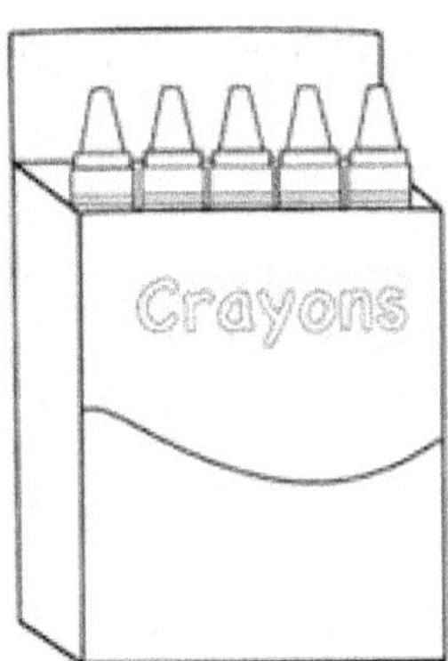

The researchers then exposed the second group to very unreliable experiences. They would offer the same larger box of crayons to each child for performing a task, but then when they accomplished whatever task they were assigned, they wouldn't provide the reward. As you can imagine, these experiences exponentially affected the likelihood a child would wait to eat the marshmallow in the follow-up test. If a child were exposed to unreliable outcomes, they would go for immediate gratification because there was uncertainty in waiting. In contrast, the kids repeatedly exposed to reliable outcomes were willing to wait for something better.

They were willing to take risks because they had experienced rewards and success in the past.

The group given a reliable and consistent experience were trained to see delayed gratification as a positive. In contrast, the second group was subconsciously trained to see it as risky and negative. As time progressed, the children that were rewarded as expected, were able to wait four times longer than their counterparts.

The children's ability to delay gratification wasn't a predetermined trait but rather based on past experiences, experiences that had emotional ties to them, like honesty and betrayal. Children that were consistently lied to lost trust. Think for a second how important that is. It doesn't matter if you are a parent or not. Understanding that how you interact with someone can affect the way they react to circumstances later down the road is significant. Whether you are a parent raising a child, an owner of a company managing your employees, a teacher, a coach, or whatever, you must take a second to realize the power your actions have on those around you.

This is just another reason why it's so important to surround yourself with the right people. Surround yourself with the right people, and your environment will produce reliable outcomes. It doesn't mean you'll always win, but it will be consistent and honest. Surround yourself with the wrong group of people, and your experiences will become unreliable ultimately encouraging you to take what's right in front of you instead of opting for more.

I want you to have the ability to pass on instant gratification. I want you to be able to defer one marshmallow for two. I want you to be able to do this because once you can pass on one now for two later, it will open up your world so that you can defer on two for fifty, and eventually fifty for a million.

Reverse Engineer Every Decision You Make

For the rest of this chapter, you will hear me use the term "value" when it comes to the decision-making process. Understand that "value" is tied to emotion. It is related to some sort of subconscious response based on beliefs or emotions like excitement, pleasure, fear, love, etc. Every decision we make goes through a series of subconscious checks that determine its priority level and, ultimately, what the outcome of that decision will be.

For most people in this decision-making process, there are just two subconscious reasons we attach "value" to performing an action or task and, in turn, make accomplishing that task a priority or not. Those reasons are 1) that we find "value" or enjoyment in the action or task itself or 2) that we see "value" or satisfaction in whatever the result is for accomplishing a given task. The first of which we will call "Task Value" and the second of which we will call "Result Value." Most people make decisions based on only these two checks. Take school, for example. If you have to write an essay, your priority level for completing the paper will first be checked by its "Task Value," or whether or not you find value or enjoyment in writing the essay on the particular subject matter.

The second check determining priority is the value or enjoyment you get from the direct result of completing the task. In this example, the direct result would be the grade you receive for completing the assignment, and in turn, the grades you receive in general at school. This is the "Result Value." People will assign "Result Value" to tasks for different reasons. In the grades example, it could be anything from wanting to please your parents because it's a necessary component to getting into college, because you enjoy the positive reinforcement from someone in particular, or a host of other reasons.

Most people make many of their decisions purely based on the "Task Value" or the enjoyment they get out of performing the action itself. This is why, as in the above example, most people "procrastinate" until the last minute when writing the essay. If a person doesn't care about the subject matter, writing the paper holds no immediate "Task Value," and so it falls lower on the priority list. The only reason it gets done at the last minute is that "Result Value" kicks in and says that, "if you don't complete this assignment, you are going to fail school," and so the average person sucks it up and completes the required task.

That's not to say there's no value in "Task Value" based decisions, because there are. The good is that the likelihood you stick to something that you enjoy doing is much higher than performing something you don't. The bad is that some of the best things you can do for yourself in the long term aren't necessarily the most enjoyable things in the world. They are often difficult and unglamorous, which means if you are only making decisions based on the task itself, this will not lead you down a path of success. The only way you will ever achieve success is if you develop enough discipline to consistently perform the things you don't want to perform.

This means making decisions such as working out, not just because you enjoy it, but because you understand the health benefits that accompany it. It means not only taking additional college courses because you like the subject matter but because it could potentially open more career opportunities. This second level of thinking and decision making takes a step forward in providing some more significant mid-to-long-term benefits because it forces us to see past immediate gratification and consider things like the consequences of a particular decision or action. This is the type of thinking that the children who were able to pass on the marshmallow had. It was why they were able to pass on the marshmallow when they were five years old and were able to continue those same behavioral patterns throughout their lives.

Most average people think the reason people work out 6 days a week and are in phenomenal shape is simply because they truly enjoy it. Those people couldn't be more wrong. Of course, those extremely fit individuals enjoy the process of working out. Of course they enjoy the added confidence it gives them. But if you think for one minute they ENJOY getting out of bed every single morning at 5 A.M., you're sadly mistaken. If you think they love eating bland chicken, vegetables, and sweet potato four times per day you are wrong. They do it because they have discipline.

There are countless mornings they are exhausted and would rather sleep in than go to the gym. There are times when they are so sick of eating healthy food it could make them puke. There are thousands of occasions where they've wanted to quit during a workout and just go home. They don't. That's the difference between them and the person who is lazy and makes excuses. It's discipline. Not motivation, discipline.

Motivation does nothing for you when you aren't motivated to get up in the morning. Motivation does nothing for you when you are sick and tired of eating the same bland food every single day. Only discipline can do that. Discipline is what successful people have. It's what fit people possess. Discipline is operating in a Result Value mindset over a Task Value mindset. It's discipline and discipline alone that allowed every single one of those kids to pass on one marshmallow so they could have two.

*Stop Being a Little B**ch*

Stop making excuses for yourself. Stop justifying and start calling yourself out on your own bullsh*t. If you don't, you'll never achieve anything you set out to do. If we give our brains enough time, we will talk ourselves out of anything. There's a great book called "The 5 Second Rule" by Mel Robbins, which basically says that you can outsmart your brain by taking action in less than 5 seconds. For example, the alarm goes off at 4 A.M. in the morning so you can head to the gym. For a lot of people, the immediate reaction is to hit the snooze button or turn the alarm off altogether and "start tomorrow." What the book tells you to do is literally count-down from 5 and force yourself to act in those 5 seconds.

It may sound dumb, but it's actually backed by scientific studies that it works. Steve-O from the Jackass movies and TV show says he has never bailed on a stunt in which he counts himself down from 3. Now, I'm not comparing you getting up at 4 A.M. to go to the gym, or finishing the book you want to write, or building out your business plan, to jumping off a 5 story building into a pool filled with dog feces, but the science behind getting someone to act is the same.

Count yourself down from 5. Tell yourself you are being a little b**ch when you are about to turn off your alarm. I'm telling you it will change your mindset immediately. You have to start calling yourself out and taking ownership of the things you are doing every day. The reality is you will have to do things you don't like if you are ever to have any hope of becoming successful. Period. You can sit there and make excuses, or you can go out and execute. If you can't manage to do that, you don't really want to change. That's the honest truth.

Remove temptation from the equation as much as possible in the same way you want to remove yourself from a negative environment. Whether it's removing cookies from the pantry so that it's not even an option to snack on at 9 P.M. or disconnecting your video game console and throwing it in the attic to remove your ability to play so that it doesn't get in the way of your side hustle.

This is how you leverage emotion. It is how you combat your mind's natural desire for immediate gratification. If you remove any possibility for instant grati-fication from the equation, the likelihood that you will then perform the tasks that provide a more significant long-term benefit will exponentially increase. If there are no cookies in the pantry to throw you off your diet, the likelihood that you will succeed will significantly increase. If your addiction to playing video games or watching a useless TV show is removed from the equation, your ability to work on something more productive will take priority because there is no al-ternative. Remove the single marshmallows from your life as much as possible.

Being able to pass on immediate gratification through discipline will be forever linked to your potential for success. It's how a business grows. You can pull more money out of your business to pay yourself a higher salary now or invest in growth so that your future payout can be far more significant. It's how you lose weight. You can eat that dessert now or have a six-pack later. It's how you succeed at literally anything in life.

The question is, if discipline is the key to value-based decision making so that you can pass on immediate gratification, what's the key element to forging that discipline? The answer is the fifth pillar of success. Businesses grow and scale because of it. It's the reason you stayed up until 3 A.M. finishing that paper in college even though you didn't want to. It's something you must implement if you want to succeed. It's a little something called deadlines, and I am going to show you how you can use them to change your life.

Chapter Nine: Become the CEO of Your Life

-The power of deadlines and raw execution-

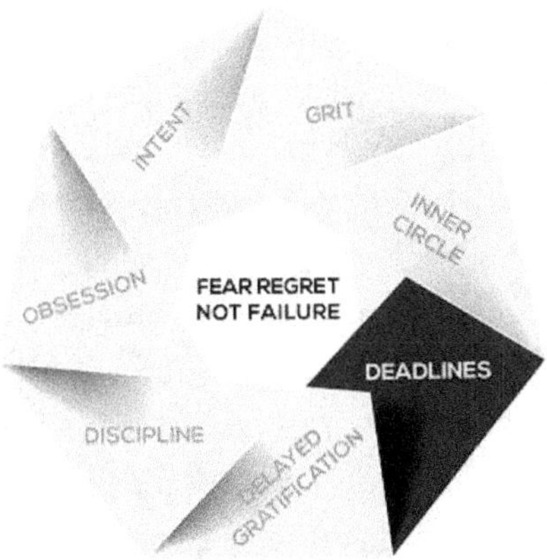

Long before Gym Rev, Afterburn, or anything else, I had an idea. A completely random idea. I am not an inventor in the slightest, but about 15 years ago, I had an idea for an invention. I had just received a ticket for not wearing my seat belt, and a day or so after, I was driving in my car thinking about ways to ensure that people didn't forget to put on their seat belts. It wasn't that I was against wearing my seat belt at the time I had received the ticket; I just had a bad habit of forgetting to put it on. So, as I drove, I pondered what could be a good way to ensure no one forgot. Then it dawned on me. Why not have something installed on a car that would prevent it from starting until the seat belt was clicked in much in the same way that you can't start a car without first pressing down on the brake.

Genius, I thought! Not only could something like this legitimately save lives, but I also felt that it could be something that would sell well. I remember thinking it was something that I could just license directly to car manufacturers, or maybe that there was an insurance play because insurance companies could offer premium discounts with something like that installed on a vehicle. The possibilities were endless, I thought!

And then the craziest thing happened, I DID NOTHING. I stopped thinking about it after a few days, and I never looked into it again. The idea faded into obscurity faster than it popped into my head. It, like 95% of all ideas, got pushed to the side. You forget about them, you start to doubt them, and you move on without ever actually executing or seeing the idea through to the end.

The story doesn't end there, though. It's only a story because of what happened next. The TV show "Shark Tank," which I am sure you have heard of, was in its very first season and one evening, I happened to be watching the second episode. All of this was about 18 months or so after that "genius" seat belt idea had popped into my head. I remember watching the show as they started to preview the next product and the person who was going to pitch it, and guess what the idea was? My seatbelt idea! The very same idea and concept I had formulated in my head over a year or two before was now being presented on a nationally syndicated TV show in front of millions of people! All I could think about was how much of an idiot I was for not having followed through.

If you can find the episode, I encourage you to watch it ("Lifebelt" season one, episode two), but to make a long story short, the guy walks out of the room without a deal because while the sharks loved the idea, they couldn't stand the guy pitching the product. He received two offers, but both involved him leaving the company and selling 100% of the business because the sharks didn't want to deal with him. Robert Herjavek put it perfectly as the guy walked out of the room, "great idea, wrong guy."

So, what the heck is the point of all of this? "Shark Tank" and seat belt inventions have nothing to do with anything that has been discussed in the last eight chapters. Or do they? This may have nothing to do with seat belts or "Shark Tank," but it has everything to do with regret and the difference between ideas and execution.

Everyone seems to want to talk about the next great idea they have. The problem is that ideas mean sh*t. An idea is only worth something if it's executed, and the problem is that 95% of ideas never get off the ground. Whether because of fear, doubt, laziness, or a myriad of other reasons, most ideas die long before they are ever given a chance to succeed. This game-changing idea I had meant nothing because I never followed through with any of it. The same applies to any idea that lacks follow-through.

Now, none of this means that had I executed that idea when it had popped into my head; I would have been the guy on "Shark Tank," crushing the pitch and walking way with a huge deal. In fact, for all I know, that guy already had the patent for it when the idea popped into my head, and my pursuit of it would have been fruitless. However, that's not the point. The point is that, while executing something doesn't guarantee victory, NOT executing something guarantees you can't win. I need you to wrap your head around that concept so tightly you never forget it. This gets to the heart of how powerful regret can be. The things that will haunt you on your deathbed are never the things you regret doing, but always the things you regret NOT doing.

Talk to any person in their 70s, 80s, or 90s and ask them what they regret. Almost no one will talk about actions taken that they regret. Instead, what you will hear are things like, "NOT spending enough time with my family," "NOT taking the chance on a business idea," "NOT calling their friend back sooner to rekindle a friendship." Almost all regrets come from the lack of action, not action itself.

The "Shark Tank" moment has resonated with me so profoundly and shaped the way I approach everything I do; not because I wish I would have become the person who had invented "Lifebelt" and become successful because of it, but because it was everything I have always believed punching me in the face, reminding me of how true regret can be when you fail to execute. I want to pass that on to you. My goal with this book is to share every failure I've had, every experience, every success, and every regret so that it empowers you never to have to feel those things, and if you have, never to feel them again.

Understand that execution is the name of the game. Without execution, success is an absolute impossibility. It doesn't matter how great an idea is. Without execution, an idea remains an idea, and nothing more. As a CEO, my job is to ensure execution on all fronts. It is to ensure that ideas become a reality. It's to impose the fifth pillar of success and the pillar of execution here in Phase Three, deadlines.

Start Acting Like a CEO

Deadlines allow a business to move forward continually, but they aren't good for just businesses. They are what will allow you to succeed in every aspect of your life. Deadlines are the biggest counter punch to procrastination, and if you aren't using them in your life, you will lose. No CEO would ever run a business without imposing deadlines. No teacher would ever be able to run a successful class without having due dates and deadlines. So, why then, do you think you will be able to run your life successfully if you don't impose deadlines on your behavior? If you want to win, then it's time you start acting like the CEO of your life instead of just a bystander.

Deadlines will be the vehicle for you to be able to execute the fourth pillar of success, Delayed Gratification, as well as the sixth pillar of success which we will discuss soon which is Discipline. Remember that delayed gratification is the act of pushing aside things you want now for the things you want two, three, ten years down the road. What this means is that without a proper set of deadlines to act as checkpoints and accomplishments, you will never be able to sustain this kind of thinking.

The only reason a teacher can ensure that most of the class turns in an assignment is that they set a deadline. The only reason a business grows is because of the deadlines and growth strategies it imposes. Just as a teacher gives deadlines, or a trainer to their client, or a manager to their employee, you must now give yourself deadlines to accomplish the smaller tasks required to achieve the big goal years down the road.

There are winners and losers in this world, and more than anything else, the one thing that separates the two is that winners execute, and losers don't. Anyone can have a great idea. The question is whether you take action on that idea or not. Anyone can aspire to lose weight and get back in shape come the new year. The difference between those who succeed and those who don't is that winners get out of bed and head to the gym when the alarm goes off 90 minutes earlier than they're used to. The difference between being part of the less than one percent of the population that achieves all of their dreams and aspirations, and the 99 percent that wake up 50 years from now wondering where their life has gone, is that the one percent executes and the 99 percent make excuses.

The most successful people in the world aren't the most intelligent. Study after study has shown that IQ on its own has little to do with success. Successful people are simply the ones who act rather than talk. They are the ones who possess persistence and determination unlike anyone else. There are millions of people who have great business or product ideas, yet most will never come to fruition. Not because the ideas are bad, but because they remain just that, ideas.

The difference between the app that gets published, or the business that gets off the ground floor, versus the ones that never launch, has nothing to do with the intelligence level of the people starting them. It has nothing to do with funding.

With enough persistence and execution, any amount of funding can be found. It's that one idea is executed, and the other is not.

The person who successfully loses 20 pounds after the holidays versus the person who fails and simply pushes it off and says, "I'll just lose it before summer" has nothing to do with one person's knowledge and experience in a gym. It has nothing to do with genetics. It's that one person executes, and the other finds excuses. It's that the person who accomplishes their goal got up when their alarm went off, and the other hit the snooze button and told themselves, "I'll start tomorrow."

Most people tend to look for excuses rather than solutions. Most people complain about the situations they are in versus actively doing what is necessary to fix the problem. The difference between winners and losers is that winners can only see the goal they are after, while losers can only see the thing that blocks their path.

The bottom line is most people give up. They lose focus. People love to say that they will just "start tomorrow," but the problem is that if you always say, "tomorrow" that day will never come. So many people trick themselves into thinking that it's ok to put off doing or starting something a day, a week, or even a month later. I want to show you how acting this way with anything, even the small things, will crush your chances at success.

The simple fact is that if you put small tasks off like the paper that's due, working out, studying, cleaning up the yard, and the dishes that are piling up in the sink, you will also do it when it comes time for essential things like talking with your child, working on your business plan, developing a great product you believe could make a significant impact on the world, or reading a book that will advance your career. The hours, days, weeks, or months you put off doing a task can very quickly become five years, ten years, or even fifty years. I promise you that if you don't figure out how to fix your issues with procrastination, your entire life will pass you by.

There is No Such Thing as Procrastination

Let's talk more about this concept of procrastination because a lot of people will blame their lack of action and execution on being a procrastinator, as though it's just a personality trait. Not only that, but they believe it's a valid excuse. They don't think it's a huge deal because, for the most part, procrastination impacts small things. It affects things like putting off the laundry. They just do it Sunday instead of Saturday. It affects the school project that they put off until the last second. The project still gets done, though, so most never see the issue with it.

The problem is that procrastination doesn't just affect those things. It will also impact the big things that can change your life. It will invade every aspect of your life because procrastination is a way of thinking; it's a mindset. Procrastination, in its most rudimentary form, is a misrepresentation of value. Procrastination is "Task Value" over everything else, and the scariest part about it is that it's subtle. That's what makes it so dangerous. It's how people become hundreds of pounds overweight.

It happens slowly over time. It's consistently putting off going to the gym. It's always making poor choices with a diet because, again, "you'll just start your diet tomorrow." It's making hundreds of tiny decisions that alone aren't an issue. Yet, the cumulative effect of procrastination is what leads the person down a path ten years from now, being 100 pounds overweight and wondering how they got there. It's what will lead you down a path where 30 years from now, you live in a state of regret because you never "got around" to writing the book you had always wanted to write.

It's a complete and utter lack of discipline, and there's a lack of discipline because there is a lack of adherence to deadlines. Procrastination is like a disease. If you don't stop it now, it will spread to the most vital parts of your life. To stop it, you first need to understand why it's happening, and more importantly, how to fix it.

Let's start this off with an exercise to highlight my point. To anyone who says they don't have time to work out or anyone who likes to "procrastinate" on going to the gym or make excuses for why they can't do it right now, listen to this. If I told you that I was going to give you $100,000 and all you had to do was wake up and meet me at the gym by 5 A.M. tomorrow, every single person reading this would be there tomorrow morning by 4:30 A.M. Why? You would have made it a priority because you value the $100,000. You would have made it to the gym when every other time you attempted it, you hit snooze.

However, just making it to the gym one day is too easy, so let's take this exercise a little further. What if, for the same $100,000, you had to wake up at 5 A.M. every day for a month to go to the gym? How many would succeed then? While there may be one or two who would fall off (shame on you), I would venture to say that 99 percent of you would make it through the month. That's far more than the approximately 5 percent who would comply if I tasked you with going to the gym at 5 AM every single day for a month with no payout. Why? Because most would prioritize the $100,000 more than the health benefits from working out.

Most would see more value in the $100,000 than in the results you would receive from going to the gym.

The same concept could be applied to the business idea you have, the book that you keep putting off writing, or the app you want to develop, but can't ever seem to "find the time." It's not that you can't find the time, it's that you CHOOSE to do something else instead because if I were to offer that same $100,000 for any of those tasks, you would miraculously find the time to do any of those things. Why? The immediate gratification of the $100,000.

You would suddenly find the time when somehow that time had eluded you for the past 12 months. It was never that there wasn't the time because we all have the necessary time. It's that you choose to sleep eight hours instead of six so you can get up early to workout. You decide to watch TV instead of working on your book. You decide to play video games instead of spending time developing that app idea you had. You decided not to research any of the hundreds of ways to get funding on the internet. Instead of calling, emailing, and driving out to meet every single human you have ever met to raise the necessary capital to fund the fantastic idea you have, you would rather go out and party. If there is something we want, the bottom line is that we make time. Procrastination doesn't exist. All that exists is our value system and the decisions we make because of it. You just lack discipline.

Understand how skewed that decision-making process is. I would argue that most people would also take a check for $100,000 tomorrow to STOP working on their business plans versus getting paid nothing to continue it. Think about how backward that is. Most would take a GUARANTEED $100,000 now versus the POTENTIAL of $1,000,000 later because of a business idea that requires hard work.

So how do you stop this? First off, understand that, like everything in life, there is no magic pill or formula. There is no guarantee of success. For everything we discuss here, A LOT is up to you. No one can hold your hand. None of the tactics we discuss will guarantee victory. All they will do is give you a tactical advantage and an increased rate of success. However, one of the most critical elements you can start incorporating into your life now to decrease the level of procrastination that exists and improve discipline is to set deadlines.

You are a Business ... Man

Businesses that are successful and able to scale have one major thing in common that their small business counterparts, solo entrepreneurs, sole proprietors, or self-employed individuals don't. Systems. It's because even though the latter is technically businesses, they don't treat themselves as such. It's because businesses have systems and deadlines, and the vast majority of individuals do not. Think about it. If you work for a company and a project is due, your boss will most likely give you a deadline. It is for that reason that the task or project is completed by that day and not a few days, a few weeks, or even a few months later. The same thing applied to you back in school. You had a paper due on Friday, and so even if you waited until Thursday night to write it, you completed it because of the due date. Of course, there were some kids in the class that may have written it earlier in the week or month, but regardless, much of the class probably waited until the last 72 hours to complete the paper.

Now imagine for a second that there were no due dates. Imagine your teacher had told you that you needed to write a paper but never mentioned that it was due Friday. The fact is that 99 percent of the people in the class would never complete the paper by Friday even though they clearly could have because they all did so when given the deadline.

What if your boss just told you to work on a project but didn't give you a due date? Most likely, it would get put off far beyond what's possible. This is the power of deadlines, and it is what allows well-run businesses to thrive. It is what separates the individual from the company when it comes to productivity. Not effectively implementing them is what is keeping you from succeeding or achieving the things you want.

If you want to start winning, you need to start treating yourself like a business. Give yourself deadlines for everything you do. Give yourself a deadline for each chapter of the book you are going to write. Give yourself a deadline to complete your business plan. Give yourself a deadline for the project you are working on for your business. Implement them, but even more importantly, follow through. This is how you develop discipline. If you don't start, you will continue on the same vicious cycle of endless procrastination without ever achieving the things you deserve. Pretty soon, 15 years will pass, and you'll wonder where all the time went.

Small victories are the key to success. Small victories are the real reason you need to incorporate deadlines. When you give yourself a deadline and a possible reward for accomplishing it, you give yourself the feedback necessary to continue onward. Remember that it is human nature to seek immediate gratification, and the only way to overcome that and instead opt for delayed gratification consistently is to have checkpoints that act like minor accomplishments along the way.

That's what deadlines are. Deadlines reinforce the reliable, consistent results that aided in the kids who opted for delayed gratification from the marshmallow test. This is how discipline is formed.

How to Prioritize Your Daily Tasks

From a psychological standpoint, it's not a lot different from something I teach and train all my managers to do. As a manager, you generally have a wide array of tasks that need to be accomplished within a given day. Those tasks have a priority level, and most people usually perform them in a most-important-to-least-important order. There is a problem with this, however. If you always complete your tasks in that order and only that order, the least essential tasks will always get pushed down the line as other new, and more important tasks come along. What ends up happening is that quite a few of those "unimportant" tasks never get done or end up taking weeks to accomplish and begin to loom overhead and cause stress and a feeling of not accomplishing anything.

If you only prioritize by the level of importance, it means that your most important task that you start your day with could be something that is going to take you hours, days, or even weeks to complete because important tasks are generally more time consuming. What this means is that you may go without any feeling of accomplishment for days or even weeks. When you operate in that manner, it will slowly eat away at your confidence, your energy, and your productivity because you fail to provide yourself with any sort of positive reliable feedback.

What I train my team to do instead is to have more of a sliding scale so that time is also a factor in how we prioritize tasks. So instead of tasks simply being performed in a

most important > semi-important > least important

order. The time it takes to complete something is also considered. That sliding scale looks a little more like what I've laid out below with that one additional variable. Each of the two variables (importance and time) is divided into three categories. Importance is broken down into; M = most important, S = semi-important, and L = least important. Time also has three categories, which are; Q = a quick solution or something that requires little time to accomplish (less than say 30 minutes), H = a solution that will take hours to complete or somewhere between 30 minutes and say three hours, and D = a solution that will take a half a day or longer to complete.

Tier 1

MQ › SQ › LQ

Tier 2

MH › SH › MD

Tier 3

LH › SD › LD

Now while the above isn't perfect and there will be times where it shifts slightly, the main take away is that the most important tasks aren't automatically prioritized to the top. In fact, time is often what dictates order. Things that can be accomplished quickly and easily take priority, with obviously the most important of those at the top of the list. Those would be your Tier One tasks. The second tier is then the rest of the especially important tasks along with the semi-important stuff that should be able to be accomplished that day. The third and final tier is the semi-important and least important tasks that require a decent amount of time to complete.

The reason for this is a sense of completion and accomplishment. Starting your day by completing (that's the keyword here) several tasks will give you a sense of accomplishment that will carry through the rest of your day. If you start with the most daunting task, whether essential or not, you could potentially go an entire day or longer without really feeling any sort of accomplishment. It's no different than why the military forces their troops to make their bed first thing in the morning. Not only does it create habits and discipline, but by doing something that seems so inconsequential, it allows soldiers to accomplish something within the first three minutes of their day, putting them in the right mindset to tackle the day that lies ahead.

These small accomplishments are what keep you motivated. They are the only things that will allow you to continue to pass on immediate gratification. If you are writing a book, don't set an unrealistic deadline of one month to complete it, or even six months. You need to trick your brain into thinking it is getting immediate gratification. So instead, create smaller goals with shorter deadlines like a single chapter by the end of the week, or even a single page by the end of the day for example. When you do that, and you follow through with it, you'll be amazed at how excited you are to repeat that same step next week.

You can do the same thing with working out. Don't set some ridiculous weight loss goal. Make it attainable. Or better yet, just make it about the act of going to the gym at the beginning. If you haven't worked out in years, don't make it 5 days or six days. Make it three days by the end of the week. Again, when you accomplish it, you will be ready for some more positive feedback and prepared to do it again the following week. No bread for a week. No alcohol for a week. Not a month, a week. But then reset and task yourself with another deadline the following week. Or better yet, simply conquer the day. No bread today. Go to the gym today. One day at a time.

There are just two requirements to this. Make it quantifiable and write it down! If you can't quantify a goal it can't be audited, and that's a problem. For example, when it comes to exercise, the wrong goal would be, "lose my belly fat." The reason is that it's super vague. I would much rather someone set a goal of "get to the gym 3x this week" or "no sugar for a week." The reason is that while "lose belly fat" sounds intriguing, there is no way to audit your success. Even if you lost 10 pounds, there is still no clear-cut answer to the goal. Knowing whether you succeed or not because you write it down is quantifiable. It is tremendously important.

Companies Set Monthly, Quarterly, and Annual Goals. So Should You.

Do the same for your business idea, your finances, whatever. Become the CEO of your life. A CEO and a company have goals and projections they want to accomplish, not just for the year, but for the quarter, the month, the week, and the day. A well-run business reverse engineers the goals of the year so they know what they need to accomplish every quarter to be able to hit that number. They know what they need to do each month to be able to hit their quarterly goal, what they need to do weekly to hit that monthly goal, and so forth. That is how a business operates; that is how a teacher or school builds out and executes a curriculum. That's how things get accomplished. There are goals, and there are deadlines to achieve those goals. Stop looking at yourself as a mere individual and start treating your life like a business, a life you are not just 100 percent in control of but are also the CEO of.

A CEO should be focused on both the long-term and short-term goals of a company just as you should be focused on your own short and long-term goals.

This is a throwback to chapter 4, and the idea that everything you do should be done with intent. This is reverse engineering, the "how" of achieving all your goals and ambitions. Remember how important acting with intent is. The deadlines you set are like checkpoints with goals and objectives. This is intent and purpose executed on a daily, weekly, monthly, and annual basis.

Break down your goals or intentions into multiple smaller micro-goals. To make this effective, you need to break down your macro goals into at least monthly and weekly goals so that they are small enough to give some level of immediate gratification when you accomplish them. If the macro goal is something that will take longer than a year to complete, then it should have yearly goals as well. This is how you develop discipline.

You are going to reverse engineer your path to achieving your goals just as a company would reverse engineer it's path. As I said a few paragraphs ago, a company knows its projections for the year and then breaks down its quarterly, monthly, weekly, and daily goals from there. All they do is ask themselves "how" they are going to accomplish that annual projection and then back in the necessary steps.

You are going to do the same thing. The first thing to do is create a deadline for accomplishing the entirety of the goal. Second, you are going to list out all the timeline or deadline checkpoints on the path to get there. The mandatory checkpoints are weekly, monthly, quarterly, and annually. You can also add in daily if you want to get hyper-focused. Once you have listed those out, you would then ask yourself how you are going to accomplish each of them within that timeframe, starting at the longest timeframe and working backward. It should look something like this.

Goal: Save $100,000 to buy a house
Deadline to accomplish: Four years
How: Save $20,000/year + Make additional $5,000/year
Annual goal: Save $20,0000, + Make $5,000 more side hustling
How: Save $1,600/month + Make additional $400/month
Monthly Goal: Save $1,600 + Make $400 side hustling
How: Save $400/week + Make $100/week side hustling
Weekly Goal: Save $400 + Make $100 side hustling
How:
Reduce going out to eat from 4 times/month to 2times, which will save $200/month or $50/week.

Save $200/month or $50/week by cutting out Starbucks.

Save $400/month or $100 week by cutting not shopping on Amazon.

Save $200/month or $50/week by canceling NFL Sunday Ticket.

Save $200/month or $50/week by reducing dates nights to 2x week instead of 4x.

Save $4,800/year or $400/month or $100/week by going from two vacations/year to one.

Save $200/month or $50/week by reducing grocery store spending by adjusting brands.

Work weekends and evenings after work, flipping stuff on eBay. If I average $10 per item, I will need to be able to flip at least ten items per week. Once you've completed this process, just as a company or CEO would, keep a calendar and track your progress. Set deadlines and ensure you are hitting your goals. It should be treated as a game that, once you start playing and chipping away at, can give you a massive sense of accomplishment that will only encourage you to continue. A CEO acts in a way that remains disciplined in sticking to the deadlines necessary to accomplish those goals. You should operate in the same way.

Or maybe you want to get to 50,000 followers on Tik Tok in six months. Reverse engineer how you get there. How many new followers would you need to average per month, per week, per day? What types of content would you need to produce? How often? What type of metrics would you need to watch, and how frequently to monitor what's working and what isn't? So on and so forth. The bottom line is that you need to lay everything out. And just like I said in the opening chapters. Write. It. Down.

Success isn't some complicated formula, but it is a formula. Success is defined by taking action and auditing the results of those actions. Success in any form comes from the willingness to do things others are not doing. The only way you will ever see success begin to form in your life is when you start treating yourself with the same level of respect and discipline with which elite athletes, CEOs, and businesses treat themselves. The fifth pillar of success, setting Deadlines, is the way you will be able to execute passing on one marshmallow for two, not just today or tomorrow, but for the rest of your life. If you don't, regret, more than anything, will begin to consume you. Stop procrastinating and stop fearing failure. Instead, fear waking up 50 years from now wondering, "what if?" Fear missed opportunity. Fear not living up to the potential you were given. If you are going to fear anything, fear regret.

Chapter Ten: Fear Regret, Not Failure

-You have one life-

Financial success has many components, but your mindset takes precedent over everything. Mindset transcends industries, it overpowers shortcomings, and it will define your actions. Mindset is everything because it is the one thing that will allow you to control and leverage your emotions instead of allowing them to overcome you. The roadblock that lines almost everyone's path and prevents success is the fear of failure. A person's ability to control and even embrace that fear is what separates those who find success from those that throw in the towel and opt for complacency.

Fear dictates so much of our lives. It's what makes our palms sweat when we peer over the edge of a tall building. It's what makes our hearts race as we work up the courage to go up to the girl or guy at the bar. It's what fills our body with anxiety when we have to speak in public. These are the conscious effects that fear has on our bodies. Yet, as impactful as these effects may seem, it is the subconscious effect it has on so many people that can dictate a person's life if they allow it.

Fear is what makes you second-guess yourself when you leave a job you hate to pursue your dream. Fear is what suffocates your willingness for change. Fear is what tricks you into choosing comfort over risk. Fear for so many people is single-handedly preventing them from achieving the success they deserve. Remember that negative emotions like fear have twice the impact on the decision-making process than positive ones, so learning to control or overcome them is crucial.

Failure is the gateway to success for absolutely everything. Learning to embrace failure is not just what separates winners from losers in the entrepreneurial space but is what separates winners from losers in almost every aspect of life. From school to business, to sports, parenting, and everything in between, the willingness to embrace failure is what allows a person to adapt and improve. It is what makes good athletes great. The willingness to embrace failure is what allowed us to learn how to ride a bike no matter how many times we fell off. It is what gives inventors the strength to continue regardless of how many times their prior attempts were unsuccessful. It is what separates the people who achieve their fitness goals and those who don't.

Practice is the Act of Putting Yourself in a Controlled State of Repeated Failure

Fitness is an easy analogy, not just because it's the main industry I do business in, but also because it's something almost every person on the planet can relate to. It's why I keep using it throughout the book. The person who works out but stops the second they become uncomfortable will never experience change. Achieving results from working out only comes from forcing yourself to the point of failure again and again and again.

The body only adapts and changes when it is under stress. The stress that induces change comes from reaching a point of failure. The people you see in your life who are in the best shape are the people who fail most often in the gym. They are the ones who push their limits each time they walk through the doors. The people who don't push themselves or who are unwilling to get outside of their comfort zones are the ones who will never change. Your mind is no different. The path to success is no different. Change, adaptation, and success in any form, only come from pushing yourself into a controlled state of repeated failure over and over again.

This is why I believe fitness is such an integral part of your success. It's not just because I am a CEO in the fitness industry; it's because I believe fitness is one of the easiest things you can do to start training your mindset. Learning to embrace failure and living outside of your comfort zone inside the walls of a gym will only assist you in being able to do so in your quest for success. Working out and learning to train to the point of repeated failure will surely change your physique, but more importantly, it will change your mind. It will be the first step in learning not to fear failure. It will be the first step in creating the confidence necessary to withstand criticism from failure. It will feed your positivity; it will provide you with a better sense of perspective; it will help build your sense of self-awareness as you learn more of who you are.

The pride that comes from the results you achieve because of your effort will provide you with a sense of gratitude and humility that motivates you to do the same thing for others around you. Working out will not just make you stronger and healthier; it will make you a better entrepreneur, a better employee, a better boss, a better parent, a better spouse, and a better friend. Learn to develop grit, determination, and resiliency in the gym, and it will only aid in your ability to apply those same things in every other aspect of your life.

It's no different than the toughness or grit that is forged in the military or in the Navy SEALS like we spoke about earlier. Any activity, physical or otherwise, that continually pushes you outside of your comfort zone and consistently tests your limits will fortify your mind to be able to withstand anything thrown your way. The thing is that you don't need to be a Navy SEAL to reap these benefits. The irony is almost every single one of us executed these things as a child every single day. It was only after some of us got older that those things faded into obscurity. It's time to bring them back.

We only learned how to ride a bike because we allowed ourselves to fail. No one gets on a bike the first time and rides around the block. Everyone falls off, everyone. It is only because of the willingness to fail repeatedly does someone finally learn the balance and skill necessary to ride without falling. It takes practice. Practice, at its core, is working in a state of controlled and repeated failure in an attempt to get better. The basketball player that is willing to put in more time developing his or her skill will advance much quicker than the one who doesn't. It is his or her willingness to miss shot after shot after shot in practice to learn what they need to adjust. It is this process of controlled failure that forces adaptation and, in turn, allows someone to make a greater percentage of shots the next time and even a higher percentage of shots the time after that.

It is this combination of ambition, discipline, and patience that allows change to occur. The ambition or desire to pursue a goal in the first place, the discipline to endure failure repeatedly because of what that continuous failure eventually produces, and finally, patience. Not as in waiting or taking your time to execute, but patience in the sense that you completely understand the process. Patience, as in knowing that anything worthwhile in life takes time. Patience, as in the discipline to pass on immediate gratification for a bigger payout down the road.

So many people are crippled by the fear of failure and other people's opinions. If you let it, fear will control you and how you react to every tough decision thrown your way. You cannot be afraid to take chances yet hope to be successful. You cannot be afraid of failure and expect to achieve greatness. Fear wants to chew you up and spit you out. Fear, more than anything, is what separates those who seize the moment from those who let opportunity slip by.

There is nothing inherently wrong with fear. Fear or doubt, as an emotion, is a normal and healthy part of being human. A person without doubts is a person without a purpose. Fear can be a powerful motivator, and if appropriately channeled, it can drive your pursuit of success. It only becomes negative when the thing driving it becomes self-sabotaging. When you fear failure, change, rejection, or the unknown, and your doubts give rise to hesitation rather than action, is when it becomes a weakness.

"So many of us choose our path out of fear disguised as practicality. What we really want seems impossibly out of reach and ridiculous to expect, so we never dare to ask the universe for it."- Jim Carrey, Maharishi University Commencement Speech

So often we deceive ourselves into thinking we are making rational decisions when the reality is that we have allowed our fear of failure to dictate our course of action. When fear is our taskmaster, what we want appears ridiculous, so we pass on it. We comfort ourselves into thinking our decisions are "logical" and "practical," when what we're doing is settling. We're taking the easy path. We stray from risk and, ultimately, our dreams because it allows us to avoid confronting our fear of failure.

We all have the potential to become great and take hold of the things we want. What separates those who achieve their legacies, versus those who find comfort in complacency is the willingness to fail. They are willing to fail repeatedly because they know that failure is a necessary part of success. They are willing to fail because they know that a person can fail at anything, even the thing they don't want. As Jim Carey famously said in his commencement speech, "you can fail at what you don't want, so you might as well take a chance on doing what you love."

Remember the thrill as a child attempting backflips off your bed or riding your bike as fast as you could down a dirt hill? Think back to that time when your fear of failure didn't exist. Think back to your childhood when your choices were governed by achievement, not fear.

As we get older, we start to realize that there can be repercussions of acting without fear. We learn that by avoiding potential hazards, we mitigate the possibility of painful consequences. We realize that acrobatics off the bed could lead to a broken ankle. We understand that riding down a dirt hill with reckless abandon may lead to hitting a pothole and going flying over the handlebars – and so we stop doing these things. Somewhere along the way, we decide to choose the safer path.

We want the path with less risk because we fear the consequences. Slowly, over time our lives become governed by the avoidance of consequences rather than the seizing of potential opportunity. We turn away from our dreams and aspirations and the potential for success because we put so much effort toward avoiding consequence and failure. Before long, we complacently give up and settle for what's safe and comfortable. We forget that broken ankles heal. We forget that no matter how many times we fell as a kid, we got up, wiped the dirt off our chests, and tried again.

We tried again and again until we succeeded because the passion for obtaining success – rather than the avoidance of consequence – filled our vision. We pushed through failure and adversity because we dreamed to, one day, be able to ride a bike instead of letting the fear of falling deter us from our goal. It didn't matter how many times we fell off our bikes, we simply got up and tried again.

This is the only way we succeed. We try, and we fail, but we try again. We try again and again until we get it right. To succeed, failure must occur. How many times did Thomas Edison fail before he got the light bulb right? How many times did the Wright brothers fail before they got an airplane to fly? The willingness to fail is paramount to your capacity to succeed. I fully understand this necessity and live every aspect of my life governed by this principle. In my office I have a poster with a quote from the great Michael Jordan. The poster is there to remind me of how important this concept is:

"I've missed more than 9,000 shots in my career. I've lost almost 300 games. Twenty-six times I've been trusted to take the game-winning shot and missed. I've failed over and over and over again in my life. And that is why I succeed."

If all your decisions were governed by fear, you would never have learned how to swim. You would have never asked your husband or wife to marry you. You have lived long enough to make decisions and take action even in the face of fear. So why now allow fear to govern decisions that involve risk? Why let your aspirations be suffocated by a fear of failure? If everyone lived with the same fear of failure that paralyzes most today, we would have never been so fortunate to witness some of the greatest athletes of all time. Explorers would never have sailed the oceans or uncharted continents. We have enough people that live their life governed by fear. Be someone who lives a life guided by their dreams. Do not be afraid to fall. Be afraid of having the capacity for flight, but never taking the leap to see if you can fly.

This is not to say that you can't or won't be afraid. If I were to tell you that I wasn't scared when I first started Afterburn Fitness, I would be lying to you. I was scared to death. I was afraid I could fail, lose everything, and have to start all over. I was fearful that I wouldn't live up to my own expectations. Yet, no matter how much fear crept into my mind, it never outweighed the fear that I would regret never having taken the chance.

The fear of failure was never enough to affect my decisions, my actions, or my future because my fear of regret was always stronger. I would rather fail 1,000 times than wake up 50 years from now, asking myself, "what if?" As long as the fear of regret outweighs your fear of failure, you will be on the path to success.

You must fear the potential regret of knowing you didn't do everything in your power to achieve all you set out to accomplish. You must fear the possible regret of knowing you could have, but you never gave yourself the opportunity. This is at the heart of everything in this book is about. There might be Seven Pillars of Success and a four-phase approach to accomplishing it all, but this is the heart. This is what pushes me every day, and I hope it can be the catalyst for you as well.

It's what I shared with you in chapter 4 about the Christmas my father was unable to afford presents. Your decisions should be governed by an overarching theme that you are driven not by the fear of failure, but by the fear of regret. Because when you are lying on your death bed 30, 50, 70, years from now, the last thing you want to feel is regret. Never forget that you only have one life. Take chances, leap for the things you never thought possible. Go out for the job you always wanted, ask the girl out at the bar, dare to chase your dreams. Remember as Jim Carey said, "you can fail at anything, so you might as well go down swinging for the things you want most."

PHASE 4: THE ONE PERCENT

Chapter Eleven: Screw Your Motivation

-Discipline is king, not motivation-

If you think motivation is going to be the thing that drives you toward success you've got another thing coming. Motivation is bullsh*t. Motivation is fleeting. Motivation is great until it fades and you no longer want to do that thing any longer. Then what? I'll tell you what, nothing. You quit, make excuses, and go back to your mediocre, complacent life. Discipline is the ONLY thing that will force you to do the things you no longer want to. F**k motivation, that what losers rely on.

Welcome to the fourth and final phase; Becoming a Part of the One Percent. In this final phase we will discuss the last two pillars of success, Discipline and Obsession, and how everything ties together. Because well, everything must tie together. You have to first understand your purpose and operate with intent in everything you do every single day.

You have to build an inner circle and an environment primed for success so that when you begin to operate that way and you undoubtedly come across struggles and failure that you have the grit and perseverance to continue on. Grit that can only be forged through discipline and an absolute obsession in achieving whatever it is you seek. Discipline and obsession which are only possible once you are able to delay gratification. Which is only possible after you create systems and deadlines that help create consistent reliable results that reinforce your actions.

That's it. That's the foundation of every successful person ever. Now of course you then have to go out and develop skills, gain knowledge, and execute every day, but it all starts here. That's how this whole thing works. No amount of motivation is going to save you at any point in this journey. Motivation is for losers; discipline is for kings.

Do you think Kobe Bryant's success was possible because he was motivated? Do you think people like the Rock's success is possible because of motivation? Do you actually think any successful business person, entrepreneur, athlete, or icon in any industry got to where they are because of motivation? No, they only got their because of discipline. There were probably a million times where Kobe Bryant, Michael Jordan, Tom Brady, or Tiger Woods were sick of practice and had no desire to go and yet they did it anyway. I'd wager that there were countless times where the Rock or Mike Tyson, or thousands of other successful people weren't motivated to wake up at 4 A.M., and yet still somehow managed to roll out of bed. Trust me when I say I operate the same way.

Their actions and mine are not predicated on some fickle sense of motivation. Motivation wanes over time no matter how strong the motivating factor is. The only way you will get anywhere in life is through discipline. And discipline comes from one central concept, responsibility.

There are many elements to discipline, but one of the biggest ways to truly grasp what it means is to understand the difference between accountability and responsibility. So much of what we have discussed is reliant on your ability to take control over every aspect of your life. Realizing that you alone are responsible for everything that happens to you is empowering beyond belief.

When you start taking control and responsibility for anything and everything in your life, you clear the way of any excuses. You eliminate the power anyone else could have on your decisions or actions when you recognize the fact that everything falls on you. The good and the bad. The successes and failures. The wins and the losses all come back to one person, you.

The part that makes this so empowering, however, isn't just that you take accountability for the things you control but that you take responsibility for everything, even the things you don't control. It's ownership of everything in your life. This critical piece eludes so many but will allow you to remain 100 percent in control of your life instead of just 50 percent. It is what distinguishes someone who searches for success from those who search for excuses. Retaining responsibility for absolutely everything that happens regardless of fault is a part of the mindset necessary to tackle life's challenges.

If you fail to maintain responsibility in your decisions or actions, you lose ownership over them. When you lose ownership over your choices and your actions, you start to lose ownership of your life. When that happens, you'll find that when life becomes difficult, you stop searching for a way to win, and you start searching for a way out.

Stop Relinquishing Power

As of the time of this writing political tensions are at an all-time high. The country is more divided than ever and both sides of the political spectrum continue to dig their heels in more and more each day. The irony is none of these constant political debates really matter all that much. Or not nearly as much as people would like to believe. The reality is that Presidents and government affect the country and the world on a macro level not a micro one. In other words, President A is not going to have a significantly better or worse impact than President B on YOUR life.

Sure, the policies they put into place may shift things a little bit and make your life 5-10% better or worse, increase or decrease your taxes a little bit, or change some law that slightly affects you, but overall they just don't affect individual lives very much if at all. The ONLY person who can create substantial long-term change in your life is YOU. The sales pitch that these politicians sell you, about how they are fighting for you and how they are going to make your life better is a political lie to get your vote. And until you realize that they will always have control over you and your life.

You have to stop relinquishing power to others and start taking responsibility not just for your actions, but in how you react to the things you don't completely control. Stop playing the damn victim. Stop complaining, stop making excuses, stop blaming the government, the man, rich people, poor people, your parents, your boss, the president, and anyone else about why your life is so damn horrible.

Wake the F up and realize that if your life sucks, it's on you and no one else. No President is going to fix that and neither is anyone else in your life. And until you realize that you will never go anywhere.

Only those willing to take 100 percent responsibility for everything in their lives will achieve all they set out to. Doing so is the only way to eliminate excuses. It's the only way to remove the potential for misplaced blame. It's the only way to be able to move forward after a loss. It's the only way to establish discipline. It's the only way for you to retain control over your life.

To fully accept 100 percent control over every aspect of your life means that if your life isn't going the way you want it to, you must come to terms with the fact that there is no one to blame but yourself. It means you give up all leverage for excuses. To have any real shot at success means that you must always remain 100 percent accountable for your actions. It means you understand that while you may not have been in control over something that happened in the past, you are always in control of what happens in the future.

The idea that the glory, as well as the failures and losses, fall solely on your shoulders is empowering but also humbling and extremely difficult. It is something that very few are ever able to accept completely. However, when you can fully commit to this concept, it will impact your decisions, change the way you view the world around you, and completely transform your life.

Everyone reading this has, at some point, heard that they need to take more accountability for their actions. What may be new to you, however, and the thing you may be struggling with while reading up to this point, is how you are supposed to take accountability for the things you can't control. How are you supposed to take accountability for absolutely everything that happens in your life when so many other factors can and will impact it?

How can, or better yet, why should the CEO of a company take accountability when an employee dropped the ball on a project and cost the company millions of dollars? How could it possibly be your fault when you were passed up for a promotion you deserved? What if you lost your job because the company you worked for went under because of Covid or something else? What accountability is there to take then? How could you possibly be at fault for being a child raised in a broken home, mistreated, or worse yet, physically or mentally abused? How could you honestly take accountability for things that you lack control of? How can you possibly take accountability for everything when other people's actions impact your life so much? And why should you?

The Power is Not in What you Can Control, but in How You React to the Things you Can't.

What if I told you that it comes down to understanding the difference between accountability and responsibility? So many people accidentally lump these two concepts together as if they are the same, but the bottom line is that they are drastically different from one another.

Most people understand accountability. Accountability is the act of holding oneself liable for their thoughts and actions, past, present, and future. It is a self-evaluation in which you honestly and objectively review and assess current and past performance. It evaluates your actions, decisions, successes, and failures, while simultaneously acting as a guideline that helps ensure follow through on all your future goals and actions.

Accountability is huge because no one else is going to watch over your actions and ensure your success other than yourself. If you cannot objectively self-evaluate and ensure follow-through, you will lose. And yet, as important as accountability is, it is still limited in its power and scope. What you are going to need in addition to accountability to succeed, is responsibility.

Even though so many people use these words interchangeably, they have one obvious distinction. Accountability only affects the things in life you have control over. But what about the actions of others that you have no power or control over? For example, there's likely no accountability you can take for a freak car accident that wasn't your fault that leaves you paralyzed. There's no accountability you can have for being raised by parents who were drug addicts. There's no accountability to be had for losing your job because the company you worked for went out of business.

Just look at the world that currently exists and how much we didn't have control over during the last two years; shutdowns, stay at home orders, and more. There are a million things we don't have control over; however, you do have a RESPONSIBILITY to yourself in how you respond to it. You must understand that while you may not be directly at fault for a particular incident, you always have a responsibility to alter the course.

A tragic accident leaving you paralyzed may not be your fault, but you have a responsibility to yourself not to let it ruin you. It's not your fault that your parents were drug addicts, but you have an absolute responsibility to yourself not to go down the same path. You have the responsibility not to use it as a crutch and affect the rest of your life. You may have no control over losing a job due to the company you work for going out of business, but you have a responsibility to get you're a** out of bed the next morning and keep moving forward.

You have an obligation and a responsibility to act regardless of fault. You can sit and make excuses, or you can realize that you have a responsibility to yourself to right the course. Even if something is completely and utterly out of your control and there is nothing you could have done. Even if no amount of accountability could have prevented such an occurrence, if there is no fault to be had, you are still responsible for acting rather than to wallow in self-pity. You still have a responsibility to execute. Not just for you, but for the ones that matter most around you. This is the kind of mindset disciplined people possess.

Most people underestimate the number of things they have actual control over. By the way, if you are a business owner, CEO, or high-level manager and you don't already operate this way, you need to start now. A true leader operates with a top-down mentality. What this means is that no matter where the actual mistake occurs along the hierarchy of a company, he or she evaluates each level above where the mistake occurred to make sure that the real culprit isn't a manager that oversees that person, a faulty system in place, or worse, you. No matter what the result of those findings, a good leader will almost always take responsibility for why it happened.

For example, if we receive a complaint from a member or client because of a poor customer service experience, the easy thing would be to reprimand that employee and move on. That's what most companies and managers do. What good companies and leaders do, however, is they audit everything in these situations. Did the manager above the employee train them properly? Do the systems we have in place give that staff member the best chance to succeed? Is the culture in that department representative of what we strive for in the company? Are they short staffed and stressed? Are the managers above those managers leading correctly and setting the right example? Am I? Are we holding all these pieces accountable and to the high standards that we set for ourselves?

These are the types of questions our management teams, and I will ask ourselves when there is an issue, and quite often, we will find a hole during the audit that needs fixing. It could be that the training wasn't thorough enough. It could be that the way we get information to our part-time employees isn't effective or efficient. The bottom line is that, quite often, it may seem as though it's the employee at fault, but in reality, it is some other aspect of the job or company that is not giving the employee the best opportunity to succeed. Ultimately that falls on our management teams and me. I have over 100 employees, and I take responsibility for all of them and their actions.

Even if when we audit everything, if it becomes clear that the employee is 100 percent at fault, then at the end of the day, guess who hired that person? My management staff or myself. Who manages this person? We do, and more than likely, it wasn't the first sign of poor performance, which means previous signs were either ignored or slipped past our radar. No matter what, that falls on us. No matter what the audit reveals, I am always taking some form of responsibility for what the root of the problem was. Not just because it's my company, but because it is the most effective way to run a business.

What if we switch roles from the CEO to the employee looking for that promotion? What if you're the employee that's been eyeing a promotion for 12 months, two years, four years? What if you get passed up by someone you're sure doesn't deserve it? Before you start blaming the system, before you blame politics or some other factor that had a hand in someone getting the promotion over you, you've got to audit yourself.

Most importantly, you need to do it honestly. Forget about what you think you know about the other employee who received the promotion over you. You have no control over what they do or don't do. All you have control over is you. Did you go over and above to get noticed? Is there anything you could have done better? Did you stay late? Did you arrive early? Were you in communication with the person in charge of the promotion long before it was up? Did you sell yourself well enough?

Or, like we're about to talk about the next chapter, were you doing the one percent of things that 99 percent of the competition isn't willing to? If there is even a fraction of a doubt, you must take responsibility for leaving even an inch open for someone else to get noticed. And even if you check all those boxes, you still have a responsibility to yourself for the next move you make rather than just wallowing in self-pity over what happened.

Just because the company's oversights caused you to lose your job or a promotion doesn't mean that you can just lie down. It doesn't mean that the obligation you have to your family, to yourself, to your future decreases. Just because you were raised in a home without a father doesn't mean you now have an excuse. It means you now have a purpose and a responsibility to be everything he couldn't be. If you've been picked on, abused, or mistreated, it's not your fault, but you certainly still have a responsibility to yourself to pick yourself up and move forward. Responsibility doesn't care whose fault it is all it cares about is that you don't just lie down and accept it. All it asks is that you not use circumstances outside of your control as a reason to quit but to persevere regardless.

Responsibility is what tells the person who has been knocked down nine times to get up ten. The responsibility to yourself in everything you do is the absolute definition of discipline. You aren't always going to be motivated. You aren't always going to want to get up early, go to the gym, write a new chapter in your book, or work on your side hustle. You are sometimes going to want to make an excuse for yourself. It is only through discipline, an ability to delay gratification and the deadlines you create to make those two things possible that anyone has any chance of success.

When you throw out the crutch to fall back on, when you trade-in searching for excuses for the hunt for solutions, you will win. Most people miss this part. Most people break at this point because they feel the world is against them. They'll say that they're cursed, but what's happening is that they're just continuing to lie down. They are not embracing the idea that no matter if you've been knocked down 37 times, you have a responsibility to yourself to get up 38. This is the way the 1% act. The 1% is obsessed while the other 99 percent lie down or make excuses. The question is, which one are you?

Chapter Twelve: Obsession

*-To become the one percent, you must do the things 99 percent of the
population is unwilling to do-*

The top one percent. A prestigious title held only by a small portion of society reaching a level of financial success, never to be accomplished by the vast majority of individuals—99 percent of them to be exact. But what does that even mean? What threshold must one cross to become a part of the one percent? The way the media describes the top one percent, you would think that the top one percent is reserved merely for the super-rich, the millionaires and billionaires.

And yet that portrayal couldn't be further from the truth. But before we get into what that threshold is to become a part of the top one percent, lets first address something that is going to be a major theme in this chapter. What it actually takes to get there.

Most people seem to understand the difficulty of becoming a professional athlete. They know the years and years of work and dedication it takes to become one of the select few who make it to the world stage. They understand the skillsets required, especially those who are aspiring to make it to the big leagues themselves. And yet, for some reason, the same appreciation and understanding seems lost when people talk about their aspirations to say, make a million dollars a year, even though the probability to achieve either is similar.

It is something that has always perplexed me. It seems like everyone has the aspirations to become a part of the one percent, but almost no one takes the actions necessary to match their ambitions. It's the equivalent of trying to become a professional athlete, but always being the last person to get to practice and the first to leave.

The probability or likelihood a high school athlete makes it the MLB, NFL, or NBA varies from sport to sport but is generally between .08 percent and .4 percent. In other words for every 10,000 high school athletes, only between 8 and 40 of them will make it to the pros while the other 9,980-ish of them end up watching it on TV like you and I. Bear in mind that those 8 to 40 people are not all superstars. Those are just people who make it. Many of whom probably play only a few years and make close to the league minimum. The ones that play for their entire career in the pros becoming household names are just a fraction of those individuals.

Okay, you probably already knew how difficult it is to achieve that. So then, what about people who already knew their chance to play for the (insert your favorite team here) expired a long time ago, but are still trying to be amongst the elusive top one percent when it comes to annual income? People like yourself. What income threshold is the mark you must achieve to become a part of the one percent? What should you set your sights on? Should it be an annual income of $1 Million? How about $2 Million? Maybe it's $5 Million? I'll tell you this. It's a lot lower than you might expect.

According to a study done in 2018, that number is just over $400,000 per year for those who live in the US. That's right, the threshold to be in the top one percent in the US is just $400k per year. Now while $400,000 a year is nothing to sneeze at, most everyone I have ever come across thought it was higher. Most people think it's at least $1,000,000, if not more. When in fact, the percentage of the population who make that much is only the top 10 percent of the top one percent or roughly .1 percent of the population. Ironically, about the same percentage as the high school athletes who make it to the pros.

So, what does all this mean? It means that not only is it extremely difficult to become a part of the top one percent, it means hitting the almighty $1,000,000/year mark (.1%) will require the same amount work, dedication, skill set, and years of perfecting your craft as it does for someone who plays professional sports. I hope that brings some perspective on what kind of work ethic elite level financial success takes. If you have audacious goals, you need to act in a manner that satisfies those aspirations.

Now the point of this isn't to crush all your hopes and dreams by making you think that achieving your goal of making $1,000,000 a year is out of your reach. Instead, it is, hopefully, to open your eyes to the work it takes to achieve that level of success in any field, whether it be starting a business, becoming a professional athlete, becoming the next YouTube star, or anything else. The bottom line is that regardless of your passion, you need to be better than 99 percent of your competition, and the only way that happens is with tremendous focus, work ethic, and the final piece of this seven-layer puzzle, obsession.

To become a part of the 1% you must become obsessed. And not just obsessed in the same way you can become "obsessed" with a girl or a guy. I'm not taking about "desire" I mean "focused" in a way only the people who actually become a part of the .1% understand. Desire, just like motivation is fleeting. Focus however, like discipline is the kind of obsession I am referring to.

This obsession must be singularly focused. One of the biggest mistakes people make when they embark on the journey of becoming successful is they hear successful people talk about things like multiple streams of income, and so they too think they should acquire multiple streams of income. What they don't understand is that is the quickest route to failure.

Think about it like this, if athlete A played baseball, football, and basketball in high school, do you think he would have a better chance of playing baseball in the major leagues if he continued trying to split his time and play all 3 of them in college and after? Or do you think he would have a better chance if he just focused on tripling down on his skillset in baseball and foregoing the other two? The answer is clearly the latter.

You and every successful person that has ever existed are no different. When successful people talk about multiple streams of income, they are only referring to acquiring those things AFTER they have mastered one and only one. You must remain obsessed with ONE thing and ONE thing only. You must become obsessed about every aspect of whatever that industry is. Tiger Woods only has so many hours in a day to practice a given craft. If he decided to split his time between golf, lacrosse, and salsa dancing, his golf game would never have elevated to the level it has.

This is the "Shiny object" concept we discussed back in chapter 4. Instead of remaining obsessed and laser focused on ONE thing and ONE thing only, people get distracted easily. Instead of focusing on just one major source of income, they begin to divert their attention away toward a second shiny object. This is a death sentence for success.

Think of it like a meal at a steakhouse. Even if you have multiple side dishes you always have a main course. The steak on your plate must always remain the center piece and focal point for everything you do. The restaurant must focus on the steak being absolute perfection. Only after the process for making the steak is perfected 1000 times over can they then focus on improving the side dishes. It's a steakhouse after-all and the reality is that regardless of whether or not the side dishes are great, if the quality of the steak begins to suffer, people will stop coming and the restaurant will go out of business. You are no different.

There are no Rainy Days

Obsession combined with discipline is your ability to do all the things you don't want to do right now, so that you may achieve all the things you dream of 20 years from now. This is what allowed me to work 80 hours a week and still come home to write the business plan for Afterburn at 11 P.M., even though I had to wake up at 4 A.M. to start to work. Obsession is what separates the greatest athletes of all time in a given sport from everyone else. Obsession is what separates the winners from the losers.

American Express ran a fantastic commercial about a decade ago on Tiger Woods. It depicted the essence of what makes great athletes great. The scene went something like this:

A camera pans through what appears to be someone's home. The light is dimly lit, and there's a warm fire going in the fireplace of the living room. You can see what looks like someone's legs wrapped in a blanket cuddled up on the couch by the fire watching TV. It's a stark difference from the scene outside. As the camera pans to a window, you can see it's cold, dark, and pouring rain. Large puddles of water are flooding the back porch. The camera pans back inside and by an office where trophies line the shelves, and a school banner hangs in the distance. The camera then moves into the kitchen and to the sliding glass door that leads to the backyard. Rain blurs your vision as it pelts the glass. In the distance, you can see what appears to be a man standing soaking wet in the middle of the backyard during the downpour. There's a bag of some kind at his feet, and he appears not to be bothered by the rain.

The man then takes a ball from the bag and places it on a tee. He lines up the head of a golf club, preparing for a shot. The camera goes into slow motion as he takes a swing. As he makes contact with the ball, the camera zooms in on the face of the man as he watches the trajectory of the ball after it flies off the tee. It's Tiger Woods. The camera stays pinned on his face as he stares intently following the path of the ball even as raindrops continue to land on his forehead. "There are no rainy days," he says.

It's a great commercial that depicts the mentality necessary to succeed. It reminds us that there are no days off if you aspire to be the greatest man to ever play the game of golf. There are no rainy days. What he and all the other athletes that sit atop their professions possess with absolute certainty is that to succeed at anything you must become utterly obsessed and focused.

If You Are Going to do Anything, Do it to the Best of Your Ability or Not at All

Obsession goes far beyond desire. It's an unwavering focus on improving every aspect of who you are to succeed in the industry it is you seek. Things like diligence, adaptability, attention to detail, and organization. These are traits that study after study after study show some of the highest correlation to success. It's why when I hire managers, attention to detail is one of the main things I look for. If someone does not appear to be detail oriented, it doesn't matter how good they are at everything else. It's deal breaker for me. After-all how can you be obsessed with anything if you aren't first extremely detail oriented?

Someone detail-oriented will follow and create systems. Someone who is well organized has a plan and knows how to execute it. Success doesn't happen accidentally. It happens when plans are executed well. It happens when you adapt on the fly. It happens when you see to it that the task you are setting out to accomplish is done well.

These skillsets are an absolute requirement because they keep your life balanced and organized during times of stress or hardship. Stress and hardship that, like we've discussed over and over, is unavoidable. You will feel overwhelmed at times. That's okay.

I have people ask me all the time. "Tony, how do I avoid getting overwhelmed?" My answer is always simple. "You don't." Just ask the CEO of a large corporation if they can avoid feeling overwhelmed. Ask a mom of four if she can avoid becoming overwhelmed. The trick isn't to attempt to create systems or refine a set of skillsets that will help you avoid feeling overwhelmed, or scared, or nervous, but rather to create systems and train skillsets that teach you how to deal with these circumstances and maneuver through them.

If you try and wait for the perfect opportunity, because you don't want to overwhelm yourself you'll be waiting forever. There's a concept you must understand. Winners play the game, and losers watch from the stands and criticize. In other words, to ever have a chance at winning, you must risk losing. You must take chances, you must be willing to fail, and most of all, you need to act. You need to stop making excuses for why you can't find the time and just execute already.

Remember that the greatest basketball players on earth couldn't dribble when they first started. The greatest minds in business were no more successful than you before they took the leap. The greatest golfers in the world swung and missed countless times before they could ever drive a ball 300 yards. Only after years of practice, sacrifice and an absolute obsession to win do the greatest basketball players of all-time wow us on the court. It's only because of their obsession to do something well that propels them to success.

Success isn't some complicated formula, but it is a formula. Success is defined by action. Success in any form comes from the willingness to do things others are not doing. It's working weekends while your friends are out partying or being the first person into the office and the last to leave. It's working for free at times because you understand that your value is not what you make per hour right now, but instead what your value will become by doing so years down the road.

Deliver Value to a Level You Didn't Think was Possible

Value is something talked about a lot nowadays. We for one, talked about it earlier in the book. However, most people don't realize what true value is, and more importantly the extreme ROI that can come from it when executed properly.

I could give you a bunch of real-life examples of companies delivering tremendous value like Amazon, Nordstrom, and others, but instead of talking in generalities with what has worked well for them, I think it's better I give you some real life examples of how we execute it at my companies.

When someone comes to tour one of our clubs, one of the critical questions our sales team is trained to ask is, "What is the most important thing for you when it comes to a gym membership?" The answers will vary wildly, but there's a very specific reason we ask that question. Not only does it give us a greater insight from a sales perspective on what could close that individual, but it also gives us a vast amount of information to execute some high-level customer service as well.

Let's say an individual's answer to that question is something along the lines of, "I've got to have a place that has nice showers and a locker room that I can get ready in every day because I work out at 5 AM and have to go to work right after." Okay, so now we know how important even something as simple as nice locker rooms and showers is to that person. What we do next is take action on that piece of information. When our sales team sets up that person's guest trial to start the following morning, they'll find out what time the guest is coming in and have a small basket of our travel size high-end shampoo and body wash, a towel, water, and a personalized handwritten card ready for them that says something along the lines of, "Hey Brian, I know how important it is to you to have a nice place to shower after your workout, so I thought I would have this ready for you this morning. Have a great workout!"

Not only did our chance to close that individual on a sale go up 10x because of the customer service they just experienced, but more importantly, it shows that we listened. I mean, when is the last time any of you experienced something like this at a gym or health club? It just doesn't happen. It's not an industry norm. It's probably something you'd more likely find in a high-end hotel, but that's exactly why we do it. Not only do we consider ourselves to be in the hospitality industry, but we want to do things that 99% of our competition doesn't do. This is just one example, but these are the ways we stand out from the competition. These are the types of things the one percent of companies do.

Small Crumbs Begin as Big Crumbs

Another example of this, and how, when you pay attention to detail, allows you to over-deliver better than 99 percent of your competition, is a story from my friend Chris whom I mentioned in an earlier chapter and who owns the catering company Locally Grown. If you remember, this is my friend who slept in his car and crappy apartments around the country while he worked free at some of the country's best restaurants so that he could learn from some of the most world-renowned chefs.

When I interviewed him as a guest on my podcast, and he was telling this story, he went on to describe his day-one experience at one of these restaurants in Chicago. During his time at that restaurant, it was Chris and a handful of other interns learning the ropes in the kitchen. It was on his first day he realized what separated great restaurants and organizations from the mediocre ones, and it all came down to attention to detail.

They had just begun their training and were prepping food for the day. As they began cutting vegetables, another intern chef who was standing right next to him had a tiny crumb of food slide off the table and fall onto the floor. The initial reaction of both the other intern and Chris was one of indifference. It was a restaurant kitchen, after all. Food, at least in small amounts, was almost certain to fall to the floor, so this seemed like no big deal to either of them. It wasn't that they were going to leave it there forever, but they figured it would just be something they could clean up later. And yet the instant the food hit the ground, the sous chef came charging over to them and told the intern next to Chris to pick up the piece of food that fell on the floor immediately, or the head chef was going to come over, lose his mind, and most likely send him home. Of course, without hesitation, the other intern immediately picked up the small piece of food off the floor and apologized, but it was the lesson from this experience that was seared into Chris' memory. A lesson that he now follows to the letter of the law when running his own company.

After reprimanding the other intern, the sous chef then broke down and reverse engineered the reason as to why that wasn't allowed. He went on to talk about how it's just one example of the importance of maintaining high expectations because what happens in the kitchen translates to the presentation and customer dining experience. If one small piece of food is allowed to fall on the floor, then one will eventually become two, and two will become 20. Pretty soon food will not only be allowed to collect on the floor, but on the countertops as well. After a while the cleanliness of the floor, the countertops, and soon the kitchen, in general, become less than desirable. If the cleanliness and the kitchen's appearance begin to falter, then soon so will the presentation of the food on the plates that go out to the customers. This means that ultimately the customer dining experience will suffer.

In other words, if food is allowed to fall on the floor and become dirty, what's to stop the countertop where the food is prepared to follow suit? And if the countertops are allowed to be less than perfect, what's to stop that same fate from affecting the foods presentation on the plate. And if the food presentation is less than perfect, so then will the presentation of things outside of the kitchen including the dining experience as a whole. The small things ultimately affect the big ones.

Chris went on to elaborate that the same mentality applied to the white aprons they wore. While you would think getting a little bit of food or sauce on your apron would be normal in a kitchen, if any of the chefs did, they were expected to change into a new, clean one or were sent home. It was explained that the reason for this was the same as keeping the whole kitchen spotless. If the chef's apron becomes dirty and the floor or counters are dirty, then the plate will never have the level of presentation it would have if the surrounding areas were pristine.

Think about it, it's not all that different than your willingness to toss something on the floor at your house if your floor is already littered with items. When your house is freshly clean you have a much lower likelihood of tossing something on the floor. You will most likely wipe the counter immediately if something spills on it. But if your floors or counter are dirty the likelihood that you don't wipe up the counter or toss something else on the floor goes up exponentially. It's just human psychology.

I experienced this last year when my wife and I moved into a new house. We are normally extremely clean individuals. I personally have a level of OCD that is almost concerning at times, but when you have boxes and stuff lining the floors and counters as you try to unpack it, is very easy to leave a bottle of water or a towel on the counter when you would normally throw or put it away. You just notice it less because it blends into the surroundings, and even my wife and I found ourselves doing this. It's human nature.

It's a snowball effect that can either work in your favor or to your detriment, depending on the standards you set. It can be a snowball that captures the essence of perfection at every step of the process and delivers a product that is second to none when you operate in a manner like the chefs and restaurant above. Or it can be a snowball that becomes the catalyst that ruins your business if you allow the little things to pile up. Remember the little things almost always become big things. Remember that crumbs matter. This is the level of obsession required to be a part of the 1%.

This is the difference between the way 99 percent of restaurants operate and how the restaurant I described operates, and the reason it is one of the most renowned in the world. It operates in a way that 99 percent of its competitors are unwilling to do. This is the level of service that the best in this world demand. It's what sets them apart from the competition. It's Amazon's Prime service, the ease, and convenience of Uber, the way you feel special when you walk into a Four Seasons hotel, the YouTube stars who engage with their fanbase, or Starbucks' willingness to remake a drink no matter the circumstances.

It's getting up at 4 A.M. when everyone else is sleeping, going to a seminar instead of the weekend trip to San Diego with your friends, and the employee who gets to work early and leaves late. It's sacrificing when others aren't willing to sacrifice. It's saving every dollar you can instead of going out to the bars or passing on the new fancy car. It's saying no to a single marshmallow now so that you can have two later.

That's the real truth here. The way you get into the top one percent is by doing all the things we have already talked about over the last eleven chapters. It's delayed gratification because passing on what you want now is what will benefit you in the future. It's operating with intent, discipline, and obsession. It's having grit so that no matter how many times you fail, you keep going. It's implementing deadlines and following through with them even when you want to do something else. It's changing the people you surround yourself with no matter how long you've been friends with them.

This kind of thinking isn't just limited to businesses. It's how you should think and operate daily. Watch how the most successful people in the world act. How long do they work? When do they wake up? When do they leave the office? What are their ACTUAL actions? Watch them and do that. What type of person are they, and how do you become that same person? What do you need to change in your life to live in the same manner? How can you operate more efficiently than 99 percent of your coworkers, and in turn, deliver better results for the company you work for? How can you look at your competition in whatever industry you are in and analyze ways to do something that 99 percent of them refuse to? This line of thinking propels people into the one percent.

If you have the audacity to want to be a part of the one percent, then you must act in a way that 99 percent of the world does not. Remember that it's not the person who sets their alarm for 4 AM that is going to win, but the person who gets their butt out of bed in the morning when it goes off. So, when you set your alarm and go to sleep tonight because you are motivated and fired up after reading this, remember that when it goes off in the morning and every ounce of your being wants to hit snooze or shut it off, ask yourself this question: What would 99 percent of the world do right now? And then do the opposite.

Chapter Thirteen: Inspire a Nation

-This is my mission-

Never during any point in our recorded history has so much opportunity been more present. Yes, even with everything that has happened in 2020, 2021, and 2022. From riots, to Coronavirus, to business shutdowns, crazy elections, war, and now the entire global economy on the brink of collapse. Even with all of that, more opportunity exists more than ever. You just need to look for it. Thanks to technology and the internet, knowledge of almost anything is only a mouse click away. Our ability to connect with nearly anyone is only a DM away.

If you want to have your voice heard, all you need to do is tweet about it. Though, sometimes, we all just need to pause and think before we tweet the latest thought that entered our headspace. Some people take this for granted, but you need to understand how much opportunity this creates. Never has the playing field between you and the large corporations of the world been leveled like this.

Back in 2005, if you wanted to become a professional photographer or editor, for example, the only real way was to go to school for it. You had to pay tens of thousands of dollars to a university or editing school. Nowadays, you can learn everything on YouTube, and it's mostly free. Back in the 90s, if you wanted to re-search a topic, you had to go to the library or get your hands on the correct volume of an Encyclopedia Britannica. If you have no idea what the Encyclopedia Britan-nica is, consider yourself young enough and lucky enough to have had information always at your fingertips. Nowadays, all you need to do is "Google it."

Before the invention of social media, if you ever wanted to attempt to get in touch with the pioneer of an industry or someone extremely successful, you had to know someone close to that person. Now all you must do is shoot them a direct message on Facebook or Instagram. You might be thinking, "Yeah, but they aren't going to respond to me," and you might be right, but what value are you bringing? Are you just asking for something, or are you offering some value or service to them at no charge? Are you doing what my friend Chris did being persistent in whatever that may be? The point is, getting in touch with high profile people isn't guaranteed, but the chance of making contact is about 1000 times more likely now than ever before in history.

In every decade prior, as a small business owner, you had almost no chance to compete from an advertising standpoint against the biggest corporations in the world. Now, because of Google and Facebook you can get your message out to anyone in the world in much the same way they do. For the first time, you can compete and have a voice. If you can't see opportunity in that, then I'm not sure if there is anything else I can say to you that will motivate you to take action.

I Want You to Win

We have covered a lot, but I need you to understand one especially important con-cept. I need you to know how much I want you to win. I need you to fully grasp how lucky we are to be alive right now and take advantage of it. I want to be able to move you and others to take action. I want to inspire a nation. I don't only want to be remembered as a successful entrepreneur; I want to do something for the rest of society, too. I want to empower everyone I meet to be the best version of his or herself and help them uncover their true potential.

Quite frankly, I just want people to be happy. I want you to be happy. I want you to be as happy as I am. To be honest, I have always considered myself a positive and energetic person, but there was something different that came over me once I discovered my purpose in life and I started to act with intent. Something changed when I began surrounding myself with people that made me better. When I started delaying gratification and setting deadlines I became disciplined. I became absolutely obsessed with every aspect of the journey and getting better. Obsessed and disciplined enough so that when I started to struggle and fail, I didn't care. I had developed enough grit that I no longer cared about what other people thought.

And through all of that I became happier. Not just because of the success that followed, but more so because I was afforded the ability to do something I love every single day. When you love what you do, work no longer feels like work.

When the thing you are good at and your passion become one it puts you in an amazing frame of mind. Its' absolute freedom plain and simple and it's exhilarating.

There's literally not a day that goes by in which I am not overwhelmingly excited to live, to go to work, to see my team, my wife, my dog, everyone. I haven't dreaded a Monday in 15 years. I don't even look forward to the weekends. Every day is equal to me. My wife jokes with me on Sunday evenings because she knows that I am just as excited for Monday as most people are for Friday. That's how much I enjoy every aspect of my life, and I want that for everyone.

It wasn't that I was an unhappy person when I was younger; it was just that I don't think I realized what true happiness was until I started to experience it. Once I did, it completely changed my entire perspective on life, and I immediately wanted everyone else to experience it. It pains me to see people that dread going to work on Monday. I hate that people have some negative view of the world or the people in it. To me, it's just a state of unhappiness, and it just seems like a miserable way to live. I want to be a part of changing that outlook on life for even one person. If I can do that with this book, then I will have won. If you aren't already there, I hope to do that with you.

Now maybe more than ever, I feel it's so important to get this message out. The world is more fractured than I can ever remember. Hatred exists along party lines, people are getting cancelled for saying anything that goes against the narrative, and if you dare to have a different opinion nowadays you are automatically labeled the enemy. We need to reunite. We need to silence division. I wish the media would just shut up sometimes. The number of negative headlines that litter our phones and televisions is starting to wear on people. We have got to make positivity louder. We have to outshine the darkness that exists in this world.

For crying out loud, we only get one life on this earth. It seems like such a waste of what is a beautiful opportunity to have it squandered. This book is about happiness in its purest form, whatever that means to you. This isn't just about success in the form of wealth creation. It's about waking up in a state of positivity every day and enjoying life even with all its challenges, heartbreaks, and losses. It is about becoming a better person and about impacting and changing the world around you. It's about stomping out fear and having no regrets.

Success isn't a Complicated Formula, but it's Still a Formula

You need to understand one important concept as this book comes to an end because it's at the heart of everything we have discussed over the past 12 chapters; success is nothing more than a mathematical equation. It is the culmination of the value you bring to the world around you. We are a transactional society, which means that we value goods and services. Those goods and services come in many forms. It can be a product that makes someone's life better or saves them time. It can come in the form of entertainment, knowledge, or inspiration.

It can be in the form of almost anything you can think of, but it has one judge and jury, and that's the free market. What is the supply and demand of whatever service or product you are bringing to the world? What is the value you bring? Can it be easily replaced or replicated? Does anyone want it?

The true currency by which our society operates is this: Value. It's why I want to push empowerment over entitlement. It's why I want to inspire you to take action rather than have you expect that something will magically come to you. The only way you will ever become successful is if you make yourself as close to irreplaceable as possible. You will only ever find success if you bring a disproportionate amount of value to others. If you look at any successful company or person, regardless of industry, there is one common denominator – Value.

Value is why the greatest athletes in the world are paid millions of dollars. It's why The Rock is the highest-paid actor in the movie industry at the time of this writing. It's the same for the music industry or any other entertainment platform. In each of these cases, these individuals are irreplaceable (or at least close to it) in their respective industries and bring value to their team owners, coaches, producers, directors, co-stars, and the end consumer. We are a society that values sports, music, movies, and television. We show it every day with our wallets.

The same goes for Amazon, Walmart, Apple, and other companies like them. If we didn't value the services or products they provide, we wouldn't spend our dollars with them. We vote with our wallets, and these companies are bringing the most value to us to ensure we vote for them. If you want to be successful, you need people to vote for you, which means that you need to bring more value to the world and the people around you than they bring to you. That's the formula, plain and simple.

The Amount of Value you bring > The Amount of Value you take

This may sound like some utopian bullsh*t philosophy but stay with me for a second because I believe this line of thinking is not only how the one percent operates but is also what will separate the winners from the losers. Plus, I want to end this book strongly, so you can't leave now. Stop thinking about what someone else owes you, what your company owes you, what your employee owes you, or what the world owes you, and start thinking about what you owe them.

A lot of people misunderstand entitlement as something that millennials or "lazy" employees possess when they look for handouts, when in fact, entitlement exists regardless of age and what side of the employment line you are on. Let me give you an example. During the hiring process at my companies, we have one specific question we ask every potential new hire regardless of position. It's a two-part question that's asked in a specific order. The first part of the question looks like this, "What do you believe you owe your employer?" Pretty straightforward, right? Most of the answers go something like "hard work," "do my best," "increase sales volume," or something along those lines.

If you think about it, most interviews are conducted entirely of questions that are just variations of this. Essentially the interviewer asks the potential employee what they can offer the company they are applying with. The employer asks questions about their experience or expertise, their accolades or performance at previous jobs, what degrees or certifications they might have, etc. The interview becomes nothing more than a "what can you do for us" series of questions, and this is where I believe so many companies go wrong. These companies forget to bring value to the employee, which is nothing more than another form of entitlement on the side of the employer. Not to mention, most people are looking for more than just a paycheck. People want to be a part of something. They don't just want to be another cog in the wheel.

I believe that interviews are a two-way street. After all, it's a mutually beneficial relationship. And yet, even though the relationship is one that benefits both parties, the interview or hiring process for 90 percent of companies is a one-sided, "what can you do for me" hot seat. Very rarely do companies do a good job selling themselves to the potential new hire (although the good ones do). The question most of these companies should be asking themselves is, why not? Why aren't they attempting to sell things to the potential new hire that makes them better than the competition down the street? Shouldn't these companies be trying to sell themselves just as much as the interviewee is attempting to sell him or herself? I mean, the entire concept of "you sell yourself 24-7" back in chapter 12 doesn't just magically stop when you are a company and conducting an interview. 24-7 means 24-7 regardless of position or title.

Think about it; it's what happens when colleges scout athletes. It's what happens when big-league teams try to hook a free agent. When colleges or professional sports teams have discussions with a free agent or athlete, they are not just looking at what that athlete or student can bring to them. They understand that part of the process is selling their school, team, culture, benefits, and city to them. It goes beyond just dollars and cents.

They understand there's more to the process of bringing someone on, outside of what that person they can do for them. They know that if they can also show what value they can provide, that individual is more likely to sign and perform well. So why then do so many businesses forego this crucial step? While I don't have the exact answer, I think that a lot of companies simply forget that the relationship between employee and employer is, in fact, a two-way street. They simply act entitled. They simply forget to provide value to the employee. And no, a paycheck isn't enough.

This is why the second part of the two-part question we ask all our new hires is, "what does your employer owe you?" Most people, when they hear this question immediately after the previous one, are hit with a slight state of shock. Most don't know exactly how to answer it at first. Not because they don't know the answer, but because they have never been asked that question or they are so taken back by it, they stumble out of the gates.

Once they regain their composure, they usually answer with, "a safe and healthy work environment," "an environment in which I can succeed," "good training," or something along those lines. Not only do we use this question to learn what motivates that potential new hire, but we use it as a lead in to be able to sell them on our company over a competitor. This is our opportunity to show that we understand that the relationship we are about to embark upon is a two-way street. This is when we show them the value that we are prepared to bring to the table.

You see, I don't just want our employees to work for my companies. I want them to WANT to work for us. I want them to WANT to come to work in the morning. I want to deliver on the things they look for in an employer. It would be selfish, egotistical, and quite frankly naïve for me to just expect them to deliver for us without us also delivering for them. It would make me no less entitled than the person that just expects success to come to them.

Not only that but when they begin to understand that we are there to give as much or more to them than they are to us, they become much more likely to dive in head-first. They become much better employees and are willing to work harder and go to battle with us because they understand that more than anything, we have our employees' backs and want to provide exceptional value to them before we ever ask anything in return.

Respect Should be Given Not Earned

I believe in giving without the expectation of return, that respect should be given, not earned. I despise the age-old saying, "respect is earned, not given." It's flat out wrong. Not because of some "politically correct" stance, I am trying to take, but because it just doesn't work. I have no interest in being politically correct just to be politically correct. I have an interest in understanding what drives human behavior. I have an interest in operating in a way that is mutually beneficial to all parties I encounter. I have an interest in winning, and this is the fast track to do so.

Not only that but to deny someone respect until they have met whatever biased standards you may have is just a cover-up for your insecurities. It's to be blinded into thinking you are operating with integrity and confidence when you are just operating out of fear. Think about it. To live by the motto, "respect is earned, not given" is to allow your fear of someone breaking or betraying your trust to govern your decisions. It is to allow your fear of someone not living up to your expectations, to prevent you from committing 100 percent. Operating that way isn't helping you, it is hindering you because you are allowing someone else to dictate your decisions and actions.

Acting this way will slow your success. If you want to win, you must break down walls. That becomes impossible, though, when you act in a way that prompts you to wait for someone else to drop their guard first because all you end up doing is fortifying those walls. I believe that when you commit 100 percent to people and start looking for ways to serve them regardless of whether they have yet to do the same, you will always come out on top. Life and the success contained within it is purely about the value you provide to the outside world. It's about removing entitlement from all sides of the equation.

It isn't just about how companies should provide disproportionate value to their employees, either. This is about you and how you can or should give disproportionate value to everyone around you as well—your loved ones, your employer, your family, and friends, etc. The person who loves unconditionally will find happiness far more often than the person who remains guarded. The company that asks what they can do for their employee before ever asking what their employee can do for them will find themselves with a team of people who are willing to go to war with them. The employee who acts in a way that seeks to learn what they can do for their company before ever asking what the company can do for them is the one who will find themselves on the fast track to promotion. The company that doesn't look to see how they can generate more revenue from their clients/customers, but instead looks to see how else they can serve and deliver more value to their clients/customers is the one that will start to generate more revenue and grow.

To the best companies in the world, the word "no" is a foreign language. They only know how to say yes. They only know how to provide extraordinary value. Nordstrom's return policy is part of that value, and what helped set themselves apart from any retail competitor in the space. For most retailers, you must have a receipt and the tag still attached if you wanted to return something. If you didn't, most places would say "no." Nordstrom's return policy, on the other hand, broke new ground in the retail industry. Don't have a receipt? Sure, no problem, we'll accept your return. Don't have the tag still and looks like you might have even worn and washed it? Sure, no problem, we'll accept your return. No receipt, no tag, you probably bought it at a different store or maybe even stole it?

Sure, no problem, we'll take it back. While that may seem like a joke, it isn't too far from the reality of how Nordstrom operates. Nowadays, a ton of other companies have adopted similar policies and have won because of it. The few dollars they might lose upfront on a return is paid back 50 times over when that person becomes a lifelong customer because of the exceptional service provided. This is the value being provided to the end consumer in its purest form, and in turn, the consumer votes with their wallet because of the extra value provided. This is how the world works. This is our currency.

The hotel industry operates in the same way. The hotel that stays strict on their policy that they don't do breakfast room service past 11 AM will never win as much the hotel company that says yes even when you call at noon. It's about service. It's about people. It's about delivering value at all times with no expectation of return. It isn't just about how businesses should interact with customers; it is also how you should operate in your own life. When you do, any potential profit that is lost immediately, or any extra hours that are invested upfront are paid out tenfold in the future.

When you, as a company, stop asking what your employees can do for you and start asking them what you can do for them is when their work ethic and loyalty will go through the roof. When you, as an employee, stop asking what your employer is going to do for you and start asking them what else you can do for them is when you will begin to knock on the door of becoming top-level management. When you stop asking what your wife or husband is doing for you and start asking them what you can do for them is when your love will become unbreakable. When your company stops saying no and starts saying yes is when you will begin to win.

Remember that no one owes you anything. Remember that life is a game of perceived value. When you can provide more value to the world around you than you take in, you will win. When you begin to provide so much value that you become irreplaceable, you will have the world at your fingertips.

If you fail to deliver a disproportionate amount of value, if you hesitate to give respect or trust openly and freely to those around you, how can you ever hope to have them fully commit to doing the same for you? How can you ever hope to have someone let down their guard if you are unwilling to drop yours? It's hypocritical, it's counterproductive, and it's the type of mentality that only fortifies the walls people inherently put up rather than breaking them down. This isn't to say that respect or trust is given indefinitely or without audit. Respect can be lost and taken away when trust is broken. You still have to set standards for what is acceptable and what's not, but that is entirely different than being unwilling to add value disproportionately in the first place.

Does living every aspect of your life, giving disproportionate value put you at a higher risk for heartbreak, betrayal, and loss? Without a doubt. But like all things in life, the bigger the risk, the bigger the reward. It's how I try to live every day of my life. Not just at work, but with my friends, my business partners, my family. It's part of how I deal with regret. It's because, just like I mentioned in the opening chapters, I feel as though I owe the world something. I want to leave my mark. I want to inspire a nation, and I want you to as well.

Be Fearless

That's the whole point of this, isn't it? To overcome fear so that you have nothing to regret. To not only win yourself but through those victories and your own actions to inspire others to do the same. It is for me. It's achieving the things you have always dreamed of while simultaneously laying the groundwork for more to follow. It's showing the world that success comes from empowerment, not entitlement. It's blazing a trail to show people that everything you dream of is possible if you put in the work.

Work. It's something that success will require of you; there's just no way around it. Unfortunately, there is no magic formula for success, only guidelines. There are only the Seven Pillars of success to guide you through the challenges that stand in your way for the journey ahead.

Success can be obtained in every industry, at any age, and regardless of circumstance. It doesn't matter whether you are passionate about real estate, finance, video games, healthcare, fitness, technology, alcohol, food, magic, music, or anything else that exists on this planet. Success and wealth can be achieved in any industry. While the path to success will vary from one person to the next, there is one constant throughout time that acts as the foundation for anyone who achieves the things they have always dreamed of: a powerful mindset.

All the talent, passion, skill, and value in the world mean nothing if you aren't mentally prepared. Your mindset is the prerequisite for success in anything. It's why you have heard the saying a thousand times, "Your mind will quit long before your body ever does." It's because it's true. The Navy SEALS are not the most decorated and skilled military unit in the world simply because they are the most well trained. It's because of the mindset they have forged over time.

Michael Jordan did not become the greatest to ever play the game of basketball because he was the best athlete of all time or because he just possessed an extraordinary skillset. Jordan was willing to lose repeatedly so he could prevail. He had one of the most competitive and driven work ethics of all time. He knew that the world owed him nothing, and the only way to achieve what he was after was to take it.

Steve Jobs and his company, Apple, failed more times than they won in the 80s and 90s. He was even fired from his own company. Most people would have given up and thrown in the towel. The only reason he was as successful as he was is that he was unwilling to give up. It was because he was willing to come back again and again and again. Only after losing for two decades did he finally win. Only because of a deep-seated passion and belief in something was he able to persevere.

None of those people expected anything from anyone, and if you ever plan to win, you can't either. You must understand that their success, mine, and your own, is not determined by some random DNA trait. It's not because one person has more opportunity than another. It is not reserved for some select few. Success is reserved for those unwilling to give up. It's for the ones that possess the Seven Pillars of success, intent, grit, inner circle, delayed gratification, deadlines, discipline, and obsession. Success is for the ones that pursue their goals as if they needed them to breathe. It's for people who bring more value to the world around them than they take. It's reserved solely for the ones who know that the world owes them nothing but are unafraid to go after everything.

Success, and the wealth and happiness that accompany it, are for those who understand their purpose. They know their why. Not just the surface level why, but the real emotional drivers behind their actions because they have taken the time to examine the pain points that will empower them to take action when leveraged properly. It's for the ones who have adopted the mentality that success is not some foregone conclusion, but instead is just a series of potential at-bats. At bats that often take a lot of swings and misses before someone is ever even able to make contact, let alone hit a home run.

This is the reality of success. The truth is that you must be willing to lose everything just to get that at-bat. Not to win, but only to have the opportunity. It is why it's so vital for you to be prepared for those opportunities should they present themselves. Not only prepared so that you take the best swing possible but prepared for what to do if you swing and miss. That's what "Fear Regret Not Failure" hopefully does for you. It prepares you to have the best chance at success and ensures you know how to react when you strike out so that you still have the strength to continue. I want it to force you to fear regret over failure.

Your success will demand that you build an inner circle filled with people that create an environment that is the most conducive for success. Remember that the people who you surround yourself with are the ones who will either encourage you to chase your dreams or hold you back. They will either help you develop things like self-awareness and self-esteem or will be the ones to break you down. They are what will ingrain things like positivity, confidence, perspective, and discipline into your life, or they will be the ones to suck those things out of you and inject negativity and entitlement instead.

Entitlement cannot exist in your world if you ever hope to achieve your dreams, for it is the antithesis of grit. Grit is what will allow you to overcome all obstacles. It is what will push you to continue, no matter how many times you fail. When you are consistently able to delay gratification by passing on one marshmallow now for two later, every decision you make will start to be about your future instead of instant gratification. When you become obsessive about the path to your goals and lay out the framework for operating with intent just as a CEO outlines the goals and projections for a company is when you start to win. When you set and execute the deadlines necessary to accomplish those tasks is when you will be on your way to becoming a part of the one percent.

*F**k Regret*

The one percent isn't some ultra-elusive dream; it's just a group of people who understand the currency our world exchanges; value. It's a group of people who take responsibility for everything that comes their way regardless of whether they have control over it or not. The 1% are just common people with an uncommon desire to be great.

When I lie on my deathbed 20, 50, 70 years from now, I don't want to wake up thinking I could have done more. I don't want to wake up thinking I could have impacted more people, achieved more of my dreams, spent more time with the people I care about, or, God forbid, that I have just wasted my life settling for some level of complacency or mediocrity because it was safe. Let me fail. Let me lose. Let me get punched in the face because that's what makes me feel alive. I want to compete until the day I die. It is the oxygen that allows me to breathe. It's the pursuit of all these things that get me up every day. I am okay giving more than I receive. I am okay risking heartbreak and loss because of it.

I want to inspire a nation. I want to give back to all those who have helped me on my journey. Only through the encouragement, guidance, and support I received did I find the will or the courage to leap in the first place. I want to be that catalyst for you. I want you to leap. It's the only way to find out what's on the other side. I promise you that when you finally build up the courage to do so, what lies beyond the cliff is worth all the struggle, heartache, and failures.

It's worth the 15-hour days and the fear of losing everything. It's worth all the free time and value you give upfront. It's worth it because it will make you happy.

It's worth it because it's the only way you'll ever know how much potential you have. It's worth it because when you live this way, regret can never come back to haunt you.

So, here's to finding out all of those things. Here's to losing. Here's to fear. Here's to your one chance on this earth. Here's to telling regret to shove it. Here's to leaping. Doing so is the only way to find out what you're capable of. It's the only way to see how great you can be. It's the only way you'll ever find out if the girl on the other side of the bar, talking to some random dude 30 minutes before the bar closes is supposed to be your wife. Here's to fearing regret, not failure.